SWITCH
IT

Published in Australia by
Destination Life

First published in Australia in 2022

Copyright © Rhonda Briscoe 2022

Rhonda Briscoe asserts the moral right to be identified as the author of this work.

All rights reserved. No part of this publication may be reproduced, stored in a retrieval system, or transmitted, in any form or by any means without the prior written permission of the publisher, nor be otherwise circulated in any form of binding or cover other than that in which it is published and without a similar condition being imposed on the subsequent purchaser.

National Library of Australia Cataloguing-in-Publication entry

A catalogue record for this book is available from the National Library of Australia

ISBN: 978-0-646-82345-4 (paperback)
ISBN: 978-0-6453117-0-9 (hardcover)
ISBN: 978-0-6453117-1-6 (ebook)

Cover desgin by Muda Grafika
Book design by Sophie White

Printed by Ingram Spark

Disclaimer: The material in this publication is of the nature of general comment only, and does not represent professional advice. It is not intended to provide specific guidance for particular circumstances and it should not be relied on as the basis for any decision to take action or not take action on any matter which it covers.

Readers should obtain professional advice where appropriate, before making any such decision.

To the maximum extent permitted by law, the author and publisher disclaim all responsibility and liability to any person, arising directly or indirectly from any person taking or not taking action based on the information in this publication.

SWITCH IT

Create a life
you love

**STRATEGIES
TO CHANGE
YOUR FUTURE**

RHONDA BRISCOE

With infinite gratitude to three beautiful, amazing men in my life:

Peter: my generous, creative husband and my forever love;

My son, James, with his soft, loving heart;

My son, Cam, who knows how to embrace life joyfully.

And warmest thanks for the support of my dearest, lifelong friends Gordana, Dori, Benita and Angie and sisters Ruth and Noela.

Thank you all for helping me 'switch' and 'shine' my life.

Special appreciation to all the people whose true stories of life appear within. Each has added greater depth to my understanding of my own journey.

Balloons of Consciousness

A MANTRA FOR ALL WHO READ THIS BOOK

I raise my consciousness and grow,

So I am more than I have been before,

The stories I have told for years, I know,

But future stories of my life speak 'More':

More Joy, more Love,
more songs of Heart and Soul

A deep awakening of a Self within,

I'm switching up my life to be more whole.

By leaving past, let present now begin.

Rhonda Briscoe

CONTENTS

	An invitation to play	10
1	Wake up and be happy every day!	15
2	Know what makes your heart sing!	19
3	To live as we would love, we first have to leave our past behind!	27
4	The Alphabet of Consciousness	32
5	A. Attitude Quotient	38
6	B. Bravery Quotient	43
7	C. Creativity Quotient	49
8	D. Determination Quotient	55
9	E. Empathy Quotient	61
10	F. Forgiveness Quotient	66
11	G. Growth Quotient	74
12	H. Heartfulness Quotient	81
13	I. Intuition Quotient	87
14	J. Joy Quotient	94
15	K. Knowledge Quotient	100
16	L. Laughter Quotient	106
17	M. Mindfulness Quotient	111
18	N. Neutrality Quotient	118

19	O. Optimism Quotient	124
20	P. Passion Quotient	131
21	Q. Questionability Quotient	135
22	R. Resilience Quotient	140
23	S. Sociability Quotient	147
24	T. Thankfulness Quotient	155
25	U. Understanding Quotient	162
26	V. Visualization Quotient	169
27	W. Well-being Quotient	175
28	X. X Factor Quotient	182
29	Y. 'Yes-ability' Quotient	187
30	Z. Zenith Quotient	191
31	Blessings	197

INVITATION TO PLAY

No one is truly able to understand our heart's desire as deeply as we ourselves. We feel and experience our lives in our unique world.

At times, we may believe life is very good and just as we would want it to be. Sometimes, through our choices, we have constructed a life that we discover to be unsatisfying. We may have even created our own disappointments and distresses without realising it, and then we have often constructed a story around these experiences that define who we have become.

This book is an invitation to go inside, often to the unconscious parts of ourselves, and take time for reflection. We may find we wish to make changes to our lives and change our pathway or our whole journey. Action may be advisable, but this is always a choice, for we will only help ourselves if we see the need to do so. And if we choose to stay in the life we are living, there is no judgement to be made. In working with some of the strategies in this book, work with friends and family by seeking feedback and trying out new, adventurous ways of personal growth.

THIS IS AN INVITATION TO PLAY

Play with options, not obligations.

Play with expansion, not expectation.

Play with possibilities, not probabilities.

Play with creativity, not certainty.

Play with joy, not judgement.

Play with many life stories, not just one.

ALPHABET OF CONSCIOUSNESS

A	Attitude Quotient	*The extent to which we understand how our attitudes influence our lives.*
B	Bravery Quotient	*The extent of our bravery in overcoming our fears.*
C	Creativity Quotient	*The extent to which we can find new solutions to problems we encounter and live creatively.*
D	Determination Quotient	*The level of motivation and energy we have to take action on a goal or decision in our lives.*
E	Empathy Quotient	*The extent to which we can see and understand another person's feelings and emotions.*
F	Forgiveness Quotient	*The capacity we have for forgiveness.*
G	Growth Quotient	*The extent to which we are flexible enough to be open to personal growth.*
H	Heartfulness Quotient	*The capacity for generosity and loving-kindness to others; our capacity to show love.*

I	Intuition Quotient	*The tendency to trust our gut feeling about people and situations.*
J	Joy Quotient	*The openness to seek joyful experiences in life.*
K	Knowledge Quotient	*The level of curiosity for knowledge in general or in particular.*
L	Laughter Quotient	*The ability to see the humorous side of life.*
M	Mindfulness Quotient	*The degree of awareness for deliberately bringing attention to experiences happening in the present moment and accepting them without judgement.*
N	Neutrality Quotient	*The ability to move into a neutral emotional position when high emotions are destructive to self or others.*
O	Optimism Quotient	*The degree to which we view the future as full of hope and with possibility for success.*
P	Passion Quotient	*The extent to which opportunity is made for doing something we love.*

Q	Questionability Quotient	*The ability to think and ask insightful questions of self and others.*
R	Resiliency Quotient	*The capacity to 'get up and get going' after a disappointment or failure.*
S	Sociability Quotient	*The ability to make and keep social connections with people.*
T	Thankfulness Quotient	*The capacity for 'living' gratitude in our daily lives.*
U	Understanding Quotient	*The ability to understand people and situations.*
V	Visualization Quotient	*The capacity to use visualization to inspire a good life.*
W	Well-being Quotient	*The ability to nurture the whole self and live with a sense of vitality.*
X	X Factor Quotient	*A quality that is hard to describe that makes someone special.*
Y	'Yes-ability' Quotient	*The degree to which we can say 'yes' to a positive life.*
Z	Zenith Quotient	*The quality of raising our awareness and actions to their highest level so we can live our best life.*

1

Wake up and be happy every day!

As one who has faced the agony of sitting at the bedside of four loved ones who died within a short number of years, I came to realise that when despair and distress strike us down, we can find understanding about life within the darkness of our deeper self.

I watched both my parents, my youngest brother and the father of my children all die grisly deaths from cancer. The journey for each one was different, but for me, each dying was like being in a cocoon of unreality as I sat daily beside them in the hospital while the rest of life seemed to bustle around me. As I went to the supermarket during these times, I would think, "These people do not know what I am going through now, that my little brother is about to die and disappear from my life forever." They were just shopping as usual, but I wondered how many of them were also experiencing their own tragedy.

Each morning, for several months, I woke up in the ocean of despair until I accepted that life was changing, and I would always have memories — good and bad memories — that needed me to switch my heart into the future and, sometimes, activate forgiveness for past hurts and disappointments. My life would keep going and I needed to translate these deaths of my loved ones into positive understandings that would help me make the most of my own life.

My experiences with the journey to death and beyond helped me gain a deeper understanding of life and enhanced my many years of professional experience as a counsellor for people in crisis. A person cannot but be forever changed by the countless sad stories of people whose lives are pitched into turmoil.

So, I learned a few important insights into life. One of those was that we may think we can be happy focusing on 'the next thing' we want or need, but so often, there is just more 'seeking' for another thing. It is so much more life-enriching to let go and leave what is not working in our lives and to "switch it" to focus on the life we can create with new thoughts, feelings and actions.

Each day, we wake up and choose happiness or discontent. We either accept the challenges of living, with all the ups and downs, or we open to fear and run for the hills! We can decide to live in our present individual paradigm of life or move forward and switch to a new life story. By changing our thoughts about our experiences, we can change our emotions and, if we do not get the life we want, at least, we may powerfully change our perspective enough to accept and even love the life we are creating.

But it is no easy journey to change our thinking, our heart's yearning, our past patterns of behaviour and our life destination. We can so often see what we need to do with our life for a new future. However, taking the leap required to change the internal conversations we have with ourselves is more than challenging; it is often debilitating. But when we start the process, a small step leads us further into ourselves. The old Chinese proverb, 'A journey of a thousand miles begins with a single step', reminds us that starting is the important part.

This is not to suggest that when catastrophe explodes in our individual world by way of illness, disablement, or death, we should immediately set feelings aside and step into the future. Rather, by first surrendering to the wounding emotional impact of grief, anger and pain, it helps us if we first fully experience our suffering. When we land in the "ocean of despair", as we all do at times, most of us swim through the rough seas and keep swimming until we reach the beach. We can then lie on the sand and feel the sunshine, first on our bodies, then in our hearts. We do not have to drown in sadness. Others may throw us a lifeline, but ultimately, we choose to switch from floating in a sea of sorrow to activating our deeper strength, an inner torch, which we switch on to light our way and save ourselves from sadness and distress. By switching our perspective on situations, we can look into the darkness, feel fear, but also activate our own capacity for rescue.

The Covid-19 catastrophe showed the world some very important learnings about what really matters. People matter. Love matters. Time matters. There is a good life for all of us when we consciously reflect on what matters and on the internal strengths which each of us have in abundance — characteristics that can aid our search for what we want and help us switch our energy onto what is most important in life. The process and practice of switching our internal conversations from the negative to the positive can awaken unconscious patterns and bring us into taking more consciously helpful actions for life.

The stories shared within this book are an invitation to journey into our own lives. What life stories are we writing for ourselves? Now? In the past? For the future? Do we consciously create our life or, maybe, let it unfold with trust in The Universe? May we be inspired to wake up each day and create a great story every day of our lives.

2

Know what makes your heart sing!

SWITCH FROM FOCUSING ON THE 'CONTENT' OF LIFE TO REFLECTING ON THE 'CONSCIOUSNESS' OF LIFE.

A wonderfully talented and sensitive young man I knew was about to begin his final year of school. His bag was loaded up with his new textbooks and computer, and his school uniform, cleaned and neatly pressed, hung on the door ready for the next morning.

But he would never wear that uniform again.

Instead, later that night, he quietly slipped out the back door and disappeared. Later, after midnight, his older brother closed up his computer to go to bed. Seeing the light in his brother's room, he decided to look in on him to check how he was feeling about the new school year. Surprised at finding him not in his room, he went searching for him...

Mitchell was still hanging from the rope he had slung over the tree. He is gone forever.

No note of farewell; no way of understanding why. His family was heartbroken, just like so many families who experienced the suicide of a loved one. So tragic!

In my lifetime, it seems as if our world has shifted from a time when we all had 'hopes and dreams' which we 'imagined' we may fulfil with the right attitude, work and natural aptitude, to a world in which our 'expectations' became imperatives that we must have what we want because we think we can, we should — or even because 'we deserve it'.

In more than forty years as a counsellor and teacher for schools, individuals and families, I have seen a gradual transition from students who seemed to believe that they could find a satisfying life pathway, despite some limitations to their capacities, to the expectation that 'you can be or do anything you want with determination and sometimes, heaven forbid, with money to buy the right education, assistant, or coach'. In the past, most people knew that not everyone could be a doctor or an engineer, a sports star or a famous singer, but that was ok because there were plenty of other life opportunities.

What is going on in this world? We have so much! But so many of us seem to feel lost, lonely and broken.

I once asked the parent of a very anxious 12-year-old boy what his strengths were, and her reply was that she thought he would be a good doctor. I thought that she was expressing her expectations for him rather than exploring his interests and strengths. I hoped that this young boy might open his mind to other possibilities when he was later choosing his future.

In my most recent years working in schools, I observed high anxiety in even the youngest students. This was together with an increasing rate of suicide as I listened to parents and students desperate to achieve "success" as they viewed it.

What does success really mean?

To each of us, obviously, it is different. Now, in our very competitive world, we strive to be "the best" in our field. Tim Costello's thoughtful book, Faith, suggests that we should 'stop comparing up as there is always someone who seems to be doing better'. He asks us to 'question what success really means' so we can be true to our own potential and 'know our inner purpose'.

Can some of us not be happy if we are simply good at what we choose to do?

Over decades, it seems we have expanded our expectations of what we want out of life yet narrowed our perspective on what measure we make of a good or successful life. We have come to seek a turbo-charged life with the goal of everything being MBB (More, Bigger, Better). We have become preoccupied with the 'Content' of life — things we wish to acquire and bring into our lives — rather than experience the 'Consciousness' of life — understandings about life as it may be.

I wonder if our society has over-valued materialism, notoriety and media perceptions of success and under-valued relationships, emotional well-being and joy-seeking.

To concentrate on a conscious life, we may need to let go of the unending search for acquiring everything we want and switch instead to reflecting on our individual life resources. Then we may open our hearts to see the full view of life around us. The photograph or picture of life which our minds have in front of us is always open and ready to be switched around and recreated with new scenes, colours and stories. The plethora of personal development books indicates that many of us are, in fact, doing just this.

For new perspectives, maybe we need new paradigms for assessing our strengths and characteristics.

The academic world has for many years used measures of IQ (Intelligence Quotient) and EQ (Emotional Quotient) for assessing the potential for people to attain 'success' in life. I have myself engaged over many years in testing students in schools to evaluate their brainpower, skills and personal attributes. By so doing, we could bring together all our testing and observations to create a summary of the strengths of each student from the information we collected. This was not a bad thing to do — it was often very helpful — but these traditional measures of our potential tended to be static and limiting. Since then, even the fixed intelligence model has been questioned by Norman Doidge (The Brain That Changes Itself) in his research which shows that the brain is more changeable than we imagined.

How exciting would it be to realise that these old traditional measures of intelligence and emotional understanding are very limiting constructs? There are many more elements which each of us can emphasize to create our lives.

While IQ and EQ measures of our individual life 'assets' have been studied and tested, often providing benchmarks for our 'success' in life, they have often limited our life story in the eyes of others and within ourselves.

In this book, you will be invited to assess other kinds of 'quotients' or measures of personal assets that you may have in abundance within you — assets that may be indicators of your ability to make the most of your life and create a satisfying life story.

These characteristics or quotients — which I have called **Consciousness Quotients** — are aspects of ourselves that can be elevated and increased by conscious reflection, deeper understanding of ourselves and relevant regular practice.

We all know tales of great people who failed at school and then created amazing lives, never limiting themselves by their school scores or failures; in fact, many believed their success was because of the failure. Not succeeding in an academic way activated other qualities such as persistence, creativity and generosity. The stories of Steve Jobs, Elton John, Bill Gates and Richard Branson, along with actresses-turned-businesswomen Cameron Diaz and Drew Barrymore, are proof that those who do not necessarily star in or even finish school, can get over their pasts and switch their lives into positive, successful futures. Even though these people are wealthy and high profile, we all know people with whom we sat in class during school days who created happy, successful lives and not necessarily with buckets of money!

Many of us have attended a school reunion where some particular 'star' has a shining success story and been praised for what they have become.

But it is more likely that our former classmates have gone on to live 'ordinary lives'. And many are living very happy ordinary lives! We all know that fame and fortune is not necessarily the best success to seek, nor does it ensure happiness. Surely, living an ordinary happy life is to be treasured.

The "Law of Attraction", espoused by many spiritual authors in Rhonda Byrne's book and film The Secret, excited us by allowing us to imagine we could all have whatever we wanted simply by asking the Universe for it. The idea of attracting into our lives what we wish for, including a new car, house, or even a lover, came with the expectation that we should have it even if it is not the best thing for us.

It is true to say that when a crisis comes crashing through the door, materialism and minor worries fly out the window.

We switch our attention.

When life and death situations arise, surely nobody thinks about that pair of red shoes they wanted last week, the new couch they felt they 'must have' or the problem with some issue at work!

People do what is in their nature to do: they worry and fret about the critical situation at hand.

They try to handle the stress and challenges confronting them. Of course, there are those who say that 'retail therapy' or a glass of bubbly is helpful, but everyone knows that the immediacy of a crisis eventually has to be faced, not avoided. On my sleepless nights, it is not those small problems that are keeping me up. I lie awake worrying about the people I love — my children, my family and my dear friends — and wish for them one thing above everything else: to be Okay in their lives. A happy and successful (by whatever definition) life would be good, but I'll settle for all of them to be happy in their ordinary lives.

The Law of Attraction is not a kind of birthday gift order to be filled, but rather an approach to living that inspires a positive and loving attitude that radiates energy from our hearts out into the Universe.

The idea of an invisible energy field around each of us is not difficult to believe when we know that fire and ice project invisible heat and cold; therefore, our energy can have a powerful 'feel' about it. It is believed that whatever energy we radiate, we get back. What we concentrate on, we attract into our lives.

Fill our hearts with hatred and revenge towards others, and our harsh energy will block goodness and happiness from coming to us.

The Law of Attraction also relies on the idea that our energy fields are all connected in such a way that this field (called the Quantum or Akashic Field) can sense our energy vibration and our heart's desires. When and if the time is right, those wishes may be fulfilled. Shamans, Yogis and Mystics, as well as many others, have accessed this 'higher consciousness', and we all can do so under suitable conditions and with deep contemplative practices such as meditation.

When people tell me that this is 'airy fairy rubbish', I have always simply replied, 'There is much scientific investigation into this field of Quantum physics.' However, if I believe in radiating positive energy into the world and it doesn't work, there has been no harm done and I have lost nothing; but if it does work, well, what amazing opportunities could come from an energy of positivity!

3

To live as we would love, we first have to leave our past behind!

Sometimes, life is not as we hoped it would be! When disappointment strikes, it's helpful to stand outside where we currently are and examine our past. We may then choose to let go of who we think we might be now in order to discover who we wish to be in the future.

We may then create a new pathway that leads to a new journey and a new — even better — story.

We all know of doctors who left the practice of medicine, lawyers who turned away from the law, and businessmen who walked away from wealth to change their lives. When we have courage to get over our past — who we have been up till now with our judgement and expectations about life — and consciously challenge ourselves, we may see that new perspectives and choices of action are a leap of faith worth taking.

Such a leap of faith saved the life of a young man who was paralysed with fear and anxiety.

He was in a grave state of mind. I knew I had to try a bold intervention to relieve him from his emotional disintegration.

It was late in the first term of school as I sat in my school counsellor's office with two parents and Jeremy (their 14-year-old son), all of us desperate to find a solution to what had become a distressing crisis. Jeremy had been dropped off at school each day of the 8 weeks of term. But each day, he would very quickly feel severely unwell and would immediately go to the school sick room. Every day, week after week, was the same. He could not physically make it to class. Medically, he had been found to be free of any particular ailment. He was a capable student, and he was socially aware, but he was increasingly unable to cope with his life at school.

School was literally making him sick.

When he was referred to me, the school nurse suspected something deeper going on. This lovely young boy was so intense and filled with anxiety that he simultaneously cried and vomited into my rubbish bin and told me he was "over life".

It was not worth living.

His father believed that it was just a case of discovering the 'problem' and finding a solution while his mother felt helpless to alleviate Jeremy's suffering.

My task was difficult. His Dad, who was paying large school

fees for his son not to attend class, was noticeably frustrated. His Mum was worried about his well-being. Interestingly, neither of them realised that the situation might end in the suicide of their son, particularly if this pattern continued.

Once they realised that this was a severe crisis and saving their son's life was a more important goal than saving his schooling, they were prepared to engage in an experiment with a drastic solution. We needed to change the pattern of his past for this was encouraging extreme anxiety that completely overwhelmed him day after day. The strategy we needed was to allow him to step out of school life as he knew it. It required that both the parents and school accept a serious alternative to attending classes.

This individual solution took two years to accomplish. But it worked! Eventually.

The plan involved taking anxious situations at school away from Jeremy, then gradually reintroducing him to the demands of his schoolwork. All he had to do was agree to come to school every day with no other expectations. He had already been attending school without going to class, so this was where we started. Easy to achieve! Then, instead of going to classes, he was to begin by choosing a subject of interest and working on it in our nearby student-friendly office space.

The goal was to alleviate his crippling anxiety. We needed to cut the current self-defeating behaviours and switch him on to a new trajectory of school life — one with no pressure.

He began by reading books and googling information of

interest, often with suggestions from me or his favourite teacher, who simply called in to see him occasionally. With all expectations and stress removed from school life, he gradually grew more relaxed and began to joke with me. He would walk to the school canteen with me on many mornings and have a hot chocolate and muffin while I enjoyed a coffee break.

He succeeded in coming to school and staying all day without being sick or feeling depressed. First Goal accomplished: stay at school!

His parents were happy but naturally very concerned about his schoolwork and what he was missing out on.

Fortunately, he had a very responsive attitude and was gradually open to attending one class per day; then the next term, two classes, and so on; until two years later, he was in full attendance and needing very little support. Because he was a capable young man and opted to pick subjects that enabled gaps in his knowledge to be managed, he then successfully completed his secondary schooling.

While his options for university courses were narrowed because his mathematics and science skills were insufficient, he was still able to find a course and future direction which he really enjoyed.

His life was changed by the switching of attitudes, expectations and behaviours of everyone in his life. This is how he learnt a new strategy to cope with life as well: reduce tasks to simple minimalist steps and cope with each before tackling the next larger task.

Start at the bottom step of the staircase — the action you can achieve — and climb up at your own pace.

While not all interventions are successful, this young man was fortunate to have supportive parents and school teachers who allowed him to take a divergent pathway through school. He was able to 'switch' his direction and change his life. Many other young people who experience problems simply drop out and end up who knows where.

WHAT ABOUT US?

Let us now take some time and assess our own personal resources.

The internal conversations we have between our heads and our hearts will benefit from being openly realised and examined with new eyes. We can then change what may not be best for our lives into behaviours that could enrich us. Let us concentrate on the 'Consciousness' of life rather than the 'Content' of life. In doing so, let us discover the possibilities of our lives and maybe, if we choose, 'switch' our direction and create our new story!

4

The Alphabet of Consciousness

Here, you will find an alphabet of concepts which make up aspects we all have in common in our lives. Sometimes, we are greatly aware of our strong character traits and sometimes not. Other people also see us differently.

By consciously reflecting on our positive aspects, we can understand ourselves and others better.

We may also learn that there is personal power in realising that change is possible. If we identify our quotient (or amount) of each element and further develop these aspects, we may 'Switch' them in ways that enhance and enrich our lives in the future.

Get to know these other **Quotients:** the aspects of ourselves that can be changed or 'Switched' if we consciously concentrate on understanding our personal level of acquisition of each characteristic and practice enhancing them.

A	Attitude Quotient	*The extent to which we understand how our attitudes influence our lives.*
		Q: How helpful are your attitudes for your life?
B	Bravery Quotient	*The extent of our bravery in overcoming our fears.*
		Q: How well do you manage anxiety and fear when difficulties arise?
C	Creativity Quotient	*The extent to which we can find new solutions to problems we encounter and live creatively.*
		Q: How creative is your thinking about your life?
D	Determination Quotient	*The level of motivation and energy we have to take action on a goal or decision in our lives.*
		Q: How well do you commit to goals and action them in your life?
E	Empathy Quotient	*The extent to which we can see and understand another person's feelings and emotions.*
		Q: How empathic are you when listening to other's experiences?

F	Forgiveness Quotient	*The capacity we have for forgiveness.*
		Q: How easily can you forgive yourself and others?
G	Growth Quotient	*The extent to which we are flexible enough to be open to personal growth.*
		Q: How open are you to seeking personal growth?
H	Heartfulness Quotient	*The capacity for generosity and loving-kindness to others; our capacity to show love.*
		Q: How open-hearted are you?
I	Intuition Quotient	*The tendency to trust our gut feeling about people and situations.*
		Q: How strong is your intuition?
J	Joy Quotient	*The openness to seek joyful experiences in life.*
		Q: How do you seek and open yourself to joy?
K	Knowledge Quotient	*The level of curiosity for knowledge in general or in particular.*
		Q: How well do you seek and find knowledge?

L	Laughter Quotient	*The ability to see the humorous side of life.*
		Q: Can you laugh at yourself easily and lighten up for relaxation?
M	Mindfulness Quotient	*The degree of awareness for deliberately bringing attention to experiences happening in the present moment and accepting them without judgement.*
		Q: How aware are you of living in the now?
N	Neutrality Quotient	*The ability to move into a neutral emotional position when high emotions are destructive to self or others.*
		Q: How well can you gain control and regulate your emotions?
O	Optimism Quotient	*The degree to which we view the future as full of hope and with possibility for success.*
		Q: How easily do you cultivate an optimistic approach to life?
P	Passion Quotient	*The extent to which opportunity is made for doing something we love.*
		Q: How good are you at making time to do what you love?

Q	Questionability Quotient	*The ability to think and ask insightful questions of self and others.*
		Q: How well do you use questions in your life?
R	Resiliency Quotient	*The capacity to 'get up and get going' after a disappointment or failure.*
		Q: How well do you recover from difficulty?
S	Sociability Quotient	*The ability to make and keep social connections with people.*
		Q: How well do you manage relationships?
T	Thankfulness Quotient	*The capacity for 'living' gratitude in our daily lives.*
		Q: How often do you count your blessings?
U	Understanding Quotient	*The ability to understand people and situations.*
		Q: How well do you understand yourself and others?
V	Visualization Quotient	*The capacity to use visualization to inspire a good life.*
		Q: How well do you visualize your future?

W	Well-being Quotient	*The ability to nurture the whole self and live with a sense of vitality.*
		Q: How do you look after your well-being?
X	X Factor Quotient	*A quality that is hard to describe that makes someone special.*
		Q: How do you explore and express your special abilities?
Y	'Yes-ability' Quotient	*The degree to which we can say 'yes' to a positive life.*
		Q: How do you embrace possibilities for enriching your life?
Z	Zenith Quotient	*The quality of raising our awareness and actions to their highest level so we can live our best life.*
		Q: How consciously aware are you of being your best self?

5

A. Attitude Quotient

HOW HELPFUL ARE YOUR ATTITUDES FOR YOUR LIFE?

I'm fine the way life is!

Michael was living a narrow, safe life. At thirty-five, with his working life well underway, he was settled in a basic, non-skilled, low-paid job even though he had a good university degree.

He couldn't risk trying for a more challenging job to match his capabilities.

He had a wife, a mortgaged house, and a car. It was a stable life, but one lived with a few friends of his own and with no hobbies in particular, apart from watching screens. He was living a predictable life, but not a joyous one. As a couple, they seemed to live their lives fairly independently. She was often frustrated by the clear, fixed views on things that lead him to rather narrow options in life.

Ask Michael how he was, and he would reply, "OK". He was not unhappy, but he hardly laughed or even smiled. Did this matter? Maybe not in his present life situation.

Sometimes people don't notice that they do not smile, or that they are unhappy.

Michael was comfortable living his life with an attitude of fixed-mindedness ('I don't want a better-paying job,' and 'I won't eat vegetables.') and an attitude that an 'ok' life was all he wanted. To others, his life seemed very unsatisfying because he lacked ambition and he limited his experiences only to those that he was prepared to try. People were ready to judge his life as meaningless. But for him, it was working out as he wanted.

*He seemed to have a present **attitude to life** that seeking a different, maybe better, life was not the choice he wanted to make at this stage — for whatever reason. If he was to keep this **attitude for life**, he might miss out on opportunities in the future. Or his wife might decide to change her attitude to him and become unhappy in the relationship. This might then lead to a decision to change or 'switch' his attitude in order to keep her happy. Or not!*

He may decide never to change his current situation. And he may keep his fixed attitudes all his life.

Michael's internal conversation between head and heart may have had a base of anxiety.

His heart may have wanted something more from life, but his head stifled him with loud messages about his inadequacy or negativity.

ATTITUDE QUOTIENT

The extent to which we understand how our attitudes influence our lives

Is our attitude to life becoming our attitude for life?

"Attitude" is a way of thinking or feeling about something. We have attitudes to everything in our lives: people, situations, ourselves, the world, life, and so on. The question to ask is whether the attitudes we have *to life* at present are leading us to fulfilling lives as we define them. If so, our attitude quotient is, for us, high. But if our attitudes to life are bringing disappointment or unhappiness, they may turn into attitudes we may not wish to keep *for life*.

The challenge is to cultivate the most helpful attitudes to enrich our life as we wish it to be. Only we can judge for ourselves the attitudes we need to have for our happiest life.

Most of us can express our approach or attitude to life by using phrases such as 'I have an "optimistic" or "adventurous" or "responsible" attitude to living' which describes our general ongoing approach and attitude to life. These are important specific attitudes that influence our everyday decisions and actions.

If we look at the bigger picture of our life journey, we may describe our attitude *for Life*, expressing it as 'I always work *to serve society in my life*,' or 'I have spent my life *focusing on creating a loving family*.' These translate into lifelong attitudes of 'service' and 'love'.

Attitude is rather like a Life Theme that comes from within us and creates our life direction. This influences our life journey.

It is obviously better for us to hold positive life-enriching attitudes rather than negative ones. A fixed attitude, for example, that prevents us from seeing any new perspective on a situation or issue can lead to roadblocks in our life pathway. A destructive attitude, which encourages someone to drink heavily or eat unhealthily, not only affects that person but also the loved ones who care for them.

When our Attitude Quotient is low because our current attitudes are not helping us live in fulfilment, what can we do to Switch them around?

SWITCH STRATEGIES: S.W.I.T.C.H. YOUR MIND, THEN SWITCH YOUR BEHAVIOURS

Suggestion: Buy a writing book and coloured pens to record your thoughts, ideas and reflections on all of the Quotients.

S **Seek a deeper understanding of your attitudes.** Write down your current attitudes to the things and people most important in your life: for example, 'My family is... (supportive?/destructive?); My work is...(challenging?/frustrating?); My home is...(comfortable?/cramped?), etc.' Get a clearer understanding of your attitudes.

W **Ways to think positively can change attitudes.** Think of ways that it might be possible to change your attitudes by looking at something positive. For example, switch the idea of 'My family is too demanding' to 'But I'm glad that they need me and love me'. Also, 'My work is challenging, but at least my colleagues are willing to help me.'

I   **Improve the attitudes that are not helping you.** Write down the Attitudes you wish to change to improve your *Life*. For example, 'I would like to approach people who are causing me to feel angry with more calm feelings and ways of speaking, instead of yelling (or holding it in with frustration).'

T   **Talk to yourself when needed.** Speak aloud a positive affirmation such as 'I am able to flexibly switch attitudes about people or things in my life if I realise that changing my thoughts and feelings will help me live a happier life.' Decide to make this affirmation an attitude you remember to think about daily.

C   **Change negative attitudes to positive.** Practice switching an unhelpful attitude (negative) to a more helpful (positive) one and get in touch with the positive energy of optimism.

H   **Help remind yourself when you fall into old habits of thought and action.** Become consciously aware of your day-to-day attitudes.

6

B. Bravery Quotient

HOW WELL DO YOU MANAGE ANXIETY AND FEAR WHEN DIFFICULTIES ARISE?

Dying? 'I'm going out dancing!'

Of the four family members I supported while they were dying, it was my mother, Nessie, who drew my greatest admiration. After an earlier brush with breast cancer, she threw herself back into life. Two years later, on her birthday, she was advised that the cancer was now 'everywhere'.

I can remember her initial shock at realising there was no hope. That death was inevitable. But what she did next amazed me!

She declared, 'If I'm going now, I'm going out dancing!' This was her way of saying, 'Bring it on!' She then took me shopping with her to buy a bright red leather coat, which she had always wanted, and a pair of purple diamante-encrusted ballet flats.

The fancy shoes would never be worn, but they were a symbol of her determination not to sit down and wait for the Grim Reaper to take her out.

From that moment, at the beginning of February, expecting only a couple of months, she proceeded to fill her calendar with many social engagements. She would slap on a morphine patch for pain and take a couple of paracetamol tablets to keep her going.

Her social activities were exhausting with lunches, movies and coffee dates most days. Never complaining to anyone, she would bravely put on her good clothes and makeup and face the rest of her life. By May, she confided to the doctor that her friends and family were so attentive and kind, and since she expected to be gone by April, she was embarrassed that she "was not dying soon enough"!

Her cancer was advancing, but her bravery and energy to live seemed to have slowed it down. On the 6th of June, she went out for coffee, lunch and dinner but woke up the next day with a terrible headache. That morning, she had a massive stroke while talking to her son on the phone.

By evening, she was gone.

It wasn't cancer that ended her life after all but a stroke!

BRAVERY QUOTIENT

*The extent of our bravery in facing
and overcoming fears and difficulties*

'Bravery' is the quality of being able to face fear, danger or difficulty with great strength. If we are brave, it means we force ourselves to try to overcome what we may fear. What we fear is different for each of us, but there are some things that most people fear. One of those is death, particularly the manner of our death.

I am sure my mother felt afraid of a gruesome death like the one she watched over as our father had suffered a few years earlier, but she faced her own demise with incredible positivity and courage. She had adult children, and this reassured her that she was not leaving dependent youngsters — for this must be the greatest fear of any mother. Nevertheless, she came home each day to sleep alone and must have endured many dark and desperate nights as she contemplated the kind of death to come. Who truly knows what gave her courage: her sense of self perhaps? An inner peace? Or just the ability to live moment by moment and one day at a time?

The existential philosopher and psychiatrist Irvin Yalom, in his book *Staring at the Sun*, explains how he believes that all anxieties come from a fear of dying. This is reinforced by many writers, and Gordon Livingston in his wonderful book *The Thing You Think You Cannot Do*, begins with the opening line: 'Death is the fundamental fear from which the others derive.' Thus, if we trace the deepest of our individual fears to their centre, it usually reveals a fear that we — or someone we love — may be hurt in some way and possibly die.

Fear is natural, of course. We all experience it to a greater or lesser extent, and it is our body and mind's warning system that helps us to be aware and look out for our safety. In extreme forms of fear, people can develop phobias, such as agoraphobia, that cripple their ability to leave the safety of their home. It takes a huge amount of bravery to face the fears that paralyse us and sometimes create illness in our body and mind. Nevertheless, even simple fears can make us so stressed and anxious, lessening our joy in life. In order to overcome the 'fear and anxiety', which is interfering with our capacity to live fully, there is nothing better to do than bravely face our fears, even little by little, and 'practice' coping and surviving them until we can trust ourselves to let them go or live with them.

In the case above, Nessie chose not to sit in her house and wait for death but to bravely face an unknown situation by embracing the fear and letting it be there but not allowing it to prevent her from living moment to moment. We can choose to back away from facing the fears that affect our quality of life or raise our awareness to the extent that we create a strategy for ourselves to increase our bravery quotient. We may well follow the advice of Susan Jeffers' book that declares: *Feel the Fear And Do It Anyway*.

When our Bravery Quotient is low because our anxiety and fears are preventing us from living in fulfillment, what can we do to Switch it up?

SWITCH STRATEGIES: B.R.A.V.E.

B **Be aware of anxiety and its effects on you.** Identify the situations in which you would like to be more courageous and/or the people whom you would like to face more bravely. Write them down. For example: 'I would like to feel less anxious about...(my children travelling to school alone/being in crowds of people/flying on a plane/speaking in public) and feel more able to overcome my fears.' Or perhaps, 'I would like to confront a colleague about their behaviours that are disturbing me.'

R **Reality of situations can be assessed.** Get to a higher understanding of the likely event that you may fear by assessing the reality of situations. People do this frequently when they have a fear of flying by saying, 'More cars crash than planes', etc.

A **Anxiety can be handled in steps.** Choose just one issue at a time that you wish to work on and come up with a series of steps, from lowest to highest anxiety-producing levels. For example, for anxiety about children travelling, steps might be: travel with them first, coaching them along the way; then find someone else they can travel with for the short term; and finally, send them alone with phone contact, etc.

V **Verify your strength by regularly speaking an affirmation:** 'I am able to recognise the fear that is causing me anxiety and to decide to practise facing and managing the fearful situation.'

E **Exercise your actions of bravery.** Consciously practice switching past behaviours around fear and anxiety, slowly building more and more bravery in situations you feel the need to manage better.

7

C. Creativity Quotient

HOW CREATIVE IS YOUR THINKING ABOUT YOUR LIFE?

Changing the world.

When I met Daniel, high up on the Indian side of the Himalayas, he impressed me as a passionate young man. In the breathtaking scenery of the mountains, philosophies of life were shared beside a campfire. It was clear that he was seeking a deeper understanding of life and the world.

His big dream was to change people's attitude towards the environment — to inspire them to change their behaviours.

He had been travelling the world for over a year seeking the very best innovative ideas to alleviate the environmental catastrophe facing his generation in the future. He searched for answers and used his website 'Changing Habits' to inspire others.

How did he fund his passion — and with very little money?

He exchanged food and accommodation for revealing and promoting each idea on his website. He had a desire to expand the knowledge of environmental options and encourage active participation in changing our habits into more sustainable practices.

I admired his enthusiasm for his cause, but even more, I marvelled at his creativity in thinking of a life option that would help achieve his greater goals while also living his dream lifestyle.

CREATIVITY QUOTIENT

The extent to which we can find new solutions to problems we encounter and live creatively

'Creativity' is the extent to which we can imaginatively find new solutions to the problems we encounter in life. It can even be new ways of seeing situations.

Many people think that creativity is a characteristic you are born with — either you have it or you don't! Of course, some people seem to have a plethora of exciting ideas and moments of genius, but if we feel rather stuck in mediocre thinking, it may be that we have not stepped outside our comfort zone and challenged ourselves.

Maybe we can learn to take our brains into new territory! For creative ideas are simply new, innovative ideas that work. We can all encourage our Creativity Quotient to expand for an exciting life.

Creativity is an energetic spark that can inspire and invigorate us. It can turn stagnation into action and regenerate us when fatigued with life. In its simplest form, it is a new solution to a problem, one that may seem different or unusual, even impractical, but which invites us to consider it. Even if the idea is not implemented, there is exciting energy in participating in creative thinking brainstorming. We all have the capacity to be creative with our lives, for it is not huge amounts of money that we need; as Daniel above illustrates, it can be small ideas that we put into practise.

What does creativity look like in our lives?

Firstly, it means seeing and doing things differently. It's not following what everyone expects of us. It's taking risks and thinking boldly. It may mean moving to somewhere we never imagined or exploring a job we didn't expect. It's breaking with tradition. When families take off and go travelling in a van for a year, or people leave good stable jobs for a change of life, they engage their creativity.

Secondly, it involves following our heart's passion. We are never so energised and happy as when pursuing something we love doing. Martin Seligman's ground-breaking research and books on happiness revealed that when we are 'in flow' — so absorbed in our activity that time passes without notice — we are happy and totally engaged. We are also most creative when 'in flow'.

Thirdly, brainstorming ideas to change our lives without judgement of them ('That's no good/That won't work', etc.) is encouraged and particularly useful when we ask others to throw their thoughts into the creative soup of ideas. This may lead to adaptation of one idea into something better.

Let us also not allow the opinions of others to sway us from stepping outside the conventional boxes, except in the case of harmful activities.

Lastly, we can feed our creative minds and hearts by seeking inspiration in nature, art and music. This allows us to remove ourselves from our immediate 'life track' and follow a short trail off to the side for relief, rest and imagination.

When our Creativity Quotient is low because our current life patterns are not helping us live in fulfillment, what can we do to Switch into a more Creative mode?

SWITCH STRATEGIES: C.R.E.A.T.E. IDEAS TO SWITCH ON OUR CREATIVE SENSES TO LIVE MORE ADVENTUROUSLY

C **Create space for Creative Thinking.** Sit in a quiet, reflective space inside or in a garden or park — wherever it feels most comfortable. Review where your life is now and ask yourself if anything is missing that you would like to find a way to bring into your future (although, keep an open mind as to when). For example, you might wish for a different job, a change of home or way of living, or to have a partner and/or family. Become aware of your intention here: is the aim to bring more leisure, love, excitement, or joy into your life? Switch on your dreams — even wild ones!

R **Reflect on life from the past, then on moving forward.** Dream big! Imagine yourself in a new life and then, working back to now, make a diagram/picture/mind map of all the steps and actions you might have taken to get there. List all the questions that you might have asked and questions and observations from others that you may have encountered. Aim for a volume of ideas without judging them. Invite a creative friend you trust to add to your ideas.

E **Explore possibilities and open your mind to believe in them by speaking an affirmation often:** 'I am able to think creatively by imagining interesting questions and seeking solutions through emptying my mind of many ideas, even playing with crazy, funny, foolish thoughts to expand my options.'

A **Amplify your dreams with intention and without judgement by the process of 'visioning'.** You may wish to explore your creativity by creating a vision board of your life on a large piece of paper with pictures, photos, words, tactile items, etc.

T **Teach yourself to be creative by consciously thinking and acting differently.** If you would normally take one pathway, choose another; or if you would mostly be conventional in your approach, explore other approaches. It can be as simple as changing something in your life in an unexpected way (e.g. Dress differently, take bold action in relationships, change the boring parts of life to exciting ways, learn a new creative skill).

E **Enjoy the process of creativity by embracing things which bring joy! Good luck!**

8

D. Determination Quotient

HOW WELL DO YOU COMMIT TO GOALS AND THEN ACTION THEM IN YOUR LIFE?

I'll do it no matter what!

Eliza, 19 years old, was homeless and living in an old car at the back of the school. She came to my attention because I was the counsellor in a co-educational secondary school at the time. One of our final year students approached me with concerns about her situation.

She was working shifts at a fast food outlet to feed and clothe herself, in order to be able to complete her schooling.

Living in a car was no life for anyone, let alone a young girl so vulnerable.

I asked her to have a chat with me, and she freely opened up about her distressing life story. When her parents separated, she was eight years old; and she remained living with her mother and younger sister but with no further contact with her father.

Eliza was excited when her mother found another partner — another Dad for her — but this turned out to be a disaster!

Sadly, for the following three years, she was sexually abused by her new father. And after confiding in her mother, she never expected to be betrayed by her. She was chastised and blamed for trying to 'cause trouble' in the family. Eliza endured the situation for far too long. It finally took a kind teacher to listen and understand her, then report the situation to the police.

What happened next will stay with me forever.

When the police came to investigate, the partner was charged despite denials; and Eliza was blamed and disowned by her mother. The police had no option but to remove Eliza from her mother and find a foster family.

She remembers leaving her house with a handful of her belongings and being taken away in the police car like a criminal. Eliza looked out the car window expecting her mother to rush out of the house and claim her out of some deep motherly love. But this never happened. She never went home again. Her mother completely rejected her! As a mother myself, I have never been able to understand this cruel action.

In the years following, Eliza lived with two foster families and severely scarred by loss, dropped out of school at 16. She almost 'checked out' of life at times but was saved by kindness from carers.

Now, three years later, a determination to finish her education and improve her life had led her to independently enrol in a local school.

Here she was then, sitting in my school office, an example of amazing determination. With substantial assistance from our school, she managed to fulfill her goal of completing the final year of school and getting into a tertiary course. What determination to achieve without the normal supports enjoyed by other students. **She dreamed, she imagined, she took action and succeeded!**

DETERMINATION QUOTIENT

The level of motivation and energy that we have to take action on a goal or decision in our lives.

'Determination' is greater than a mental decision to do something we want to do; it is an emotional connection to the goal or action we wish to embrace. It is the degree of energy in the emotion that stimulates and guides us towards our achievements.

Unfortunately, determination to do something, while usually helpful to us, can also be destructive, for just as we may have consciously positive goals such as 'getting fit' or 'passing exams', we may also have unconscious behaviours which sabotage our goals. Addictive habits like alcoholism, smoking and poor nutritional food choices can be engaged with intense determination.

Let us focus here on positive determination as a quality to improve our lives.

The degree of energy and motivation we are prepared to enlist to achieve our goal or dream is proof of our determination. Eliza, above, was prepared to do whatever it took to return to school, even when she was homeless. The question we can ask ourselves to assess our Determination Quotient is: 'How much do I want this and what am I prepared to do to make this happen?'

Determination is required for two kinds of goals: firstly, the ones we dream of achieving, such as owning a house or getting a new job and secondly, the goals we have to achieve for some other purpose, such as finishing a task at work. Effort expended on the first is often enjoyable and motivating; working on the second is frequently tiresome and boring. The second is often also necessary as a prelude to acquiring the first; for example, saving money for the house we want.

Stephen Covey's powerful self-help book, *The 7 Habits of Highly Effective People*, was written 30 years ago, but it remains a classic which is still highly relevant today. It shows clearly how we can achieve much by simple practices that work. Keeping 'the end in mind' is one very helpful strategy.

When our Determination Quotient is low because our current life goals and actions are not helping us to be where we hope to be, what can we do to Switch up our determination?

SWITCH STRATEGIES: G.O. F.O.R. I.T!

G **Goals make a difference!** Create and select one of a number of goals that you wish to achieve, then list the steps/actions needed to accomplish this. Be clear about the specifics of the goal — what, when, how and why? — and rate it out of 10 as to how much you want it. (If it is only desired to the level of 3, question whether it's worthwhile actually working for.)

O **Open your visioning mind often!** Switch on Determination by visualising the end goal. Let your mind and heart never forget what you are working for because it's the reason for spending significant time and energy out of your lifetime.

F **Find a cause for Celebration!** Motivation is Determination's bedfellow; they need each other! Each step towards the goal must be completed, ticked off and celebrated as motivation for the next step and the gradual march toward the final accomplishment.

O **Old patterns and behaviours of apathy can be changed.** To switch our thinking, we need to consciously be aware of the times when lack of determination is holding us back and decide to shake it off by starting with one small action forward. Practice switching. Be in control of what you wish to be!

R **Remember that repeated affirmations can powerfully strengthen our resolve**. When I was a young, eager student of music and I had many examinations to pass, I would play Beethoven's Eroica Symphony as motivation and determination to do well. I created words of affirmation to go with the melody of the first movement: 'I can, I will, I know I can! I can, I will achieve whatever I want to!' Along with hard work, my affirmation worked to create some amazing results that I had dreamed of in my mind. Louise Hay, one of the most prolific spiritual and personal development authors of our time, was the master of 'Affirmations'. She advocated saying them aloud as often as possible for personal encouragement.

An affirmation for Determination might be: 'I can do this!' Speak and repeat often.

I **Inspire yourself by imagining how you will feel when you achieve what you dream about.**

T **Talk to yourself about not allowing yourself to be a victim of your thoughts.** When determination falters, pick yourself up with straight talking to your heart and get back into it. No excuses!

9

E. Empathy Quotient

HOW EMPATHIC ARE YOU WHEN LISTENING TO OTHERS' EXPERIENCES?

Feelings from Death.

When my former husband died of cancer 8 years after our twenty-year marriage had ended, I found myself suddenly saddened and tearful.

He was no longer important in my life although he was still involved with our two children. But there was a miasma of conflicting feelings that I needed to reflect upon.

My close friends did not assume that I would react in any particular way; instead, they tried to unearth my swirling emotions. By asking me questions about how I was feeling and truly listening to my heart's emotions, they helped me understand my reaction better. Without any judgement from them, I was able to express conflictual feelings arising from good memories of the past overlaid by distressing memories.

I then discovered my emotions were arising from a blend of sadness, relief and regret.

The empathic response from friends was to try to help me examine and express my feelings by entering my world through listening deeply and then trying to understand whatever feelings I might experience. It is a powerful skill worth developing.

EMPATHY QUOTIENT

The extent to which we can see and understand another person's feelings and emotions

'Empathy' is a quality that is so important for our relationships. It is a vital key to understanding our family, friends and work colleagues and very important in enriching our own emotional vocabulary. Its Greek derivation means 'in feeling', and the idea is to imagine that we could stand in someone else's shoes and understand how that person feels and experiences their situation.

The value of empathy is that people we relate to in any sphere of our lives will trust us more and share more of themselves because they feel we really understand them without judgement. Someone with the characteristic of high empathy is seen as warm and caring in the eyes of others.

When we feel 'sympathy', we feel sadness for someone, and this is helpful; but the focus is on how 'we' feel about their situation not on understanding how 'they' are feeling. Empathy is deeper; it is the ability to imagine how someone else experiences a situation from their standpoint. In the circumstance like that above, a person may tell us someone has died, and we may identify sympathetically, imagining how we might feel. We may even assume another person's feelings are the same as ours — which they may be — but they may be completely different. There may be a range of conflicting feelings, as in the situation above.

How another person responds to a situation can be revealed if we ask questions and listen carefully, showing empathy. Empathy does not judge other people's reactions and feelings; it simply listens attentively to understand.

When our Empathy Quotient is low, we can learn simple strategies for increasing our innate sensitivity to others' emotions and also gain a better understanding of ourselves

SWITCH STRATEGIES: F.E.E.L.

F **Find the emotion.** Since Empathy is all about identifying and experiencing emotions, we can increase our understanding by expanding our consciousness of our own feelings and becoming more observant of others.

- Take moments in each day to be still, and reflect on the feelings you have been experiencing, giving them a label and a context. Check in with yourself to make sure of the feelings. For example, 'I've been feeling tired and bored (feelings) this morning at work, but maybe it's because I am disappointed that

I didn't get the promotion I wished for (checking in with other feelings).'

- Observe people all around you and try to identify their emotions and similarly, label them. Practice with the people you love or with friends by observing and commenting, even asking a question to check out the feelings. For example, 'You seem rather distracted and agitated today? Are you annoyed about something?'

E **Express the emotion freely.** Open your heart to expand the feelings you are experiencing and without judgement, feel into the ways of expressing those feelings.

- Do you need to weep and feel sorry for yourself for a while?

- Do you need to feel and express anger in a private place or with a trusted friend?

- What might help in the short term? And what might bring relief in the longer term?

When understanding other people or helping someone you care for to release emotions, consciously take any of your own judgement out of your observations. Keep a neutrality about other people's feelings and actions so they do not feel negatively judged but rather understood and accepted. Listen to their heart's feelings and show them your empathic response by stating your observation and showing care and understanding. For example: 'I understand you felt angry with your friend for letting you down and not apologising.' (Understanding without judgement.) Compare this with the judgemental shutdown statement: 'Feeling angry with your friend is a waste of energy. It wasn't that bad!'

E **Expand your understanding of emotions.** Go out into nature and invite adventures in art and music to expand your heart. Especially, seek experiences that create feelings of awe, for these are the richest, most fulfilling emotions we can know for increasing our capacity for empathy.

L **Listen with your heart.** A simple affirmation might be: 'I know I can expand my feelings and truly tune in to the emotions of others by observing and listening with my heart.'

10

F. Forgiveness Quotient

HOW EASILY CAN I FORGIVE MYSELF AND OTHERS?

*Forgiveness is necessary
for true peace of mind*

Amanda, Olivia and Jake were in their early teens when their father and mother separated. They were devastated. Their Dad loved them — and their mother dearly — and had wanted to remain married, but his wife was determined to end the marriage and to convince their children that he was their enemy.

For many years, he lost contact with his children.

Their mother had told them so many untruths: that they were poor, and their father had deserted them financially and emotionally; also, that he didn't love them. This was devastating and destructive for young children.

In fact, he had not only continued to pay private school

fees for each of them together with weekly payments, but he had also left his family with a beautiful house, another beach house and a rental apartment — more than five million dollars in assets.

He left himself with nothing except his business.

But their dishonest mother convinced them that it had been her who had supported them. What could the manipulated youngsters do to please their mother? They adopted her intense hatred and vengeance, refusing to see their father. They could not forgive him for what they had been told he had done.

Despite him trying desperately to keep contact and to continually make loving overtures to his children, his former wife's festering hatred and contempt poisoned them against him.

It was not until they were in their early twenties that their father was able to reconnect with them and prove he had never neglected them or stopped caring about them. It took the shocking event of an attempted suicide by his son to create a window, through counselling, for him to come back into his children's lives. When they realised they had been infected by their mother's lies and vengeance, they turned against her and did to her exactly what had been modelled to them: they filled themselves with fury and blame.

In this tragic circumstance, the mother's hatred and desire for the destruction of her former husband were overwhelming. She could not forgive him for not being who she thought he should be. As a consequence, she ended up destroying the lives of her whole family for many years, perhaps forever.

There is an old saying that warns us, 'Revenge is like drinking poison in the hope that it will kill your enemy.' Lack of forgiveness, or worse, the determination not to forgive, is tantamount to deciding to put needles in our own shoes and walking with the pain constantly.

FORGIVENESS QUOTIENT

The capacity we have for forgiveness.

Forgiveness is the conscious decision to release feelings of resentment, anger or vengeance towards others or sometimes, towards ourselves.

It does not mean forgetting and excusing any person's actions. But releasing ourselves from carrying emotions that can disturb, even destroy, our peace of mind and health is taking care of ourselves.

Forgiveness is one of the most essential of life attributes to possess but unfortunately, it is also one of the most challenging qualities to acquire.

Why is this so? It is because the most highly charged emotions we can experience are often connected to this characteristic. We have all felt so angry with someone that we have wished for revenge, and some of us have been so grief-stricken by an event that it seems like the people involved can never be forgiven.

Elton John's song, 'Sorry Seems To Be the Hardest Word', rings true for each of us at some time during our life. We can feel the emotion in the words:

> *It's sad, so sad*
> *It's a sad, sad situation*
> *And it's getting more and more absurd...*
> *It's sad, so sad,*
> *Why can't we talk it over...*
> *Sorry seems to be the hardest word.*

Wayne Dyer, the very wise, renowned author of a vast number of personal development books reveals *How To Forgive Someone Who Has Hurt You in 15 Steps*. This is a vital resource for anyone who struggles with forgiveness. One of his most important messages is to 'switch the focus from blaming others to understanding yourself'.

Even more complexity is involved when we realise forgiveness may not just require forgiving others but also forgiving ourselves. Accepting our 'human-ness' requires that we first have to develop a conscious understanding of our deepest dark emotions. We have to become aware of our 'Shadow' side: the parts of ourselves that we reject or do not want to face.

Releasing negative self-judgement when we feel we are to blame is another huge undertaking. After a terrible event or situation, we have all agonised with the words, 'If only I had....'

Then, there is the condemnation of others whom we blame for our negative feelings. How often do we fail to let go of the wrongs that others do to us? This is such a challenge. We may need to choose to release ourselves from the constant drinking of poison through reliving hurt and anger which only serves to bring us more suffering. There are a few certainties in life which we all must remind ourselves about often:

1. The past is past and cannot be changed: to keep focusing on it is to destroy the present and future. Better to live in the now and change how we think about the past. Even the most horrendous or tragic circumstances and events must be felt fully in grief and eventually released into the past where they can sleep.

2. The only person we can consciously change is ourselves and even that means we must want to change. We may put huge effort into changing someone else, but it is pointless and frustrating if that person is not motivated to do so as well.

3. We will all face the end of life at some stage, and living in states of anxiety, anger and suffering is detrimental to our health.

To improve our capacity for forgiveness, we first have to truly understand how much power is in the capacity to forgive.

Blame, judgement, hatred and revenge are devastating emotions that insinuate themselves into our minds, hearts and souls. But allowing them to grow and fester there like mould will send peace of mind, happiness and joy fleeing away fast.

Our personal energy field will also emit negative energies

which repulse those within our field. Live in hatred long enough and we can never have peace of mind; alternatively, live with a loving, generous spirit and we will attract positive energy and experiences into our lives.

The deep emotional work created by Brandon Bays in The Journey book and workshops reveals how much the process of forgiveness is a deep internal experience and can change lives by allowing forgiveness to bring life-changing emotional freedom.

When our Forgiveness Quotient is in need of expansion, we can help ourselves with some helpful practices.

SWITCH STRATEGIES FOR FORGIVENESS: REVEAL. REVIEW. RELEASE. REMEMBER

REVEAL the hurt, disappointment and distress that is being felt by speaking about it with a trusted friend, counsellor, or if possible, the person who is the cause of the distress. It can also be written down, creatively expressed in art or music if any of these mediums are personally helpful. (After all, so many songs, poems and paintings are a cry from the heart of their creator.) Seek feedback from others regarding their viewpoints and be prepared to consciously uncover the deepest feelings and especially, notice where they are felt in the body (e.g. stomach, heart, head, etc.).

REVIEW the people you need to forgive including every person, feeling and memory affecting your peace of mind and causing you heartache. It may or may not help to write this down. Choose one that is most disturbing at present and decide to participate in a Forgiveness Action Ceremony to release and let go of this hurt, pain, disappointment and/or suffering.

RELEASE and let go with a Forgiveness Action Ceremony. The purpose of this active release is to create a collection of activities that are personally meaningful and appropriate to you and your situation. This is all about becoming consciously aware of both the expressed and/or suppressed emotions that are continuing to influence our lives.

Design a creative ceremony that might involve some of the following activities:

- Candle lighting – to symbolically shine light on the situation; to represent the element of fire; to indicate a beginning or end of a ceremony.

- Post-it notes or large sheets of paper to write names of people related to the hurt or angst and/or events related to these. These notes can even be burnt in the candle flames later or shredded in a symbolic gesture to release negative emotions and events.

- Speaking aloud an affirmation such as 'I am able to identify the events and people whom I need to forgive so that I reach a feeling of acceptance and can release the debilitating effects of the negative emotions.'

- A time of meditation in which there is a visioning of the release of the hurt and pain out of the body. This can be imagined as being sent out into the air, burnt into an imaginary campfire, or sent floating away in the water. There are many wonderful meditations for healing and forgiveness on the internet to help with this step also.

- After the release of negative emotions, action is needed to express both the intention to forgive and the healing power of forgiveness. For example, natural objects such as rose petals, pebbles, leaves or flowers may be scattered while repeating words such as 'I forgive…(name of person) for…(hurtful action), and I summon my strength for a courageous and happy future life.'

REMEMBER to remind yourself to release and forgive over and over, as often as needed going forward. It is easy to slip into old patterns, so it helps to be conscious of the need to reconnect with feelings of forgiveness and keep reinforcing the healing power. If courage to forgive fails (as it will now and again), giving rise to the old negative and self-destructive feelings, bring those feelings to full consciousness and choose to let them go and visualise them releasing physically into the ether. Consciously choose peace of mind each day and eschew anger and revenge that can only lead to misery and anguish.

11

G. Growth Quotient

HOW OPEN TO SEEKING PERSONAL GROWTH ARE YOU?

Courage to change the pathway of pain to follow the uncertain pathway of passion.

As tears welled in his eyes, Lucas' heart was breaking. Here was a delightful and engaging seventeen-year-old, who had come into my counsellor's office halfway through his final year of school, just after the mid-year exams.

He had only passed 3 of 6 subjects and had failed the main science studies needed to get into the Engineering course for which he had been aiming over many years. He had passed three humanities subjects because he had good writing skills. His sense of failure was overwhelming him, and he was nervous about telling his parents, who had made quite high sacrifices to pay for large private school fees. What the hell am I going to do now? My parents expect me 'to succeed in life by getting a good job'.

When I reflected on his subjects, I commented that he seemed to be good at humanities and asked him if he had chosen the subjects like chemistry, physics and the most difficult maths because he liked them or simply as prerequisites for a course. His downcast weeping eyes looked up at me and he murmured, 'I hate these subjects and I don't even want to do them. It's what my parents want me to do!' I asked him if he had a passionate interest.

What he said next was the beginning of a life-changing personal growth journey with an amazing outcome!

'I want to sing and perform in operas and musicals!' he exclaimed. I tried out for the school production of Mikado (Gilbert and Sullivan) and got the lead role and I just love everything about it! He was not even doing any music subjects!

A week later, I sat in the school auditorium, absorbing his chocolatey-smooth tenor voice and brilliant acting, stunned at his talent (as a former opera singer myself, I thought I had good judgement). I asked him if he would be prepared to drop the science subjects, study the lowest maths and take up the option of singing as a music practical subject for the School Certificate, with a view to auditioning for the University School of the Arts Performance Program. He had no idea of this as a possibility.

So he did this, finally with his parents' approval, and worked hard on the music subject, achieving a pass in the other three subjects. Despite a mediocre yearly result, his audition was so stunning that he gained entry to a top course. He worked hard and completed a music degree. Four years later, I received an invitation to his first major professional singing engagement, singing the tenor role in Monteverdi's Vespers. And his professional performing career continues. Well done, Lucas, for being prepared to change your life!

GROWTH QUOTIENT

The extent to which we are flexible enough to be open to personal growth

Often it is a crisis, as in the case of Lucas above, that necessitates a new life direction. Sometimes, it is a feeling of stagnation, of being stuck in a circular life trajectory, or worse, embedded in the quicksand that stirs us into action to change our lives, step onto a new path and choose a journey of change and personal growth. If Lucas had actually used his clever mind and worked hard on his science subjects, he may have followed the path he was on, only to live a life without passion and adventure. If life jogs along happily, we have no reason to seek personal growth, so when stagnation, boredom, emotional pain and suffering get a grasp of our hearts, we can either give up and go into hiding, simply accept life as it is, or bravely bring the challenges into consciousness and begin to change direction.

Tragedy is often the most painful but most dramatic inspiration for personal growth as we know. Gordon Livingston, author and psychiatrist, who lost his two children within seven months of each other, one to suicide and the other to leukemia, writes: 'We are, after the loss of someone we love, like soldiers who have been pinned down in combat: afraid to move but knowing that, if we do not, our lives are over'. His book, *The Thing You Think You Cannot Do*, reveals how, in the face of dire circumstances beyond our control, we can shut down our future and complain about the world, or we can find some pathway through personal growth into a new life. Because tragedy changes our perspective on life, choosing to step tentatively forward will result in personal growth, whether expected or not; but even without tragedy, by seeking openness to change, we can choose to enrich our experience of life. Furthermore, we intensify our opportunity for personal growth by communicating our vulnerability to those people in our lives whom we trust. Sharing our feelings and our fears and receiving empathy, insights and love from our nearest and dearest, brings comfort in difficult times, and it also encourages them to share their own life journeys of tribulation and of wonder. There is an old saying that 'the biggest room in the world is the room for improvement', so opening up to personal growth can improve every aspect of our lives.

When our Growth Quotient is low and we wish to increase our propensity for personal growth, there are many worthwhile actions that will provide inspiration

SWITCH STRATEGIES FOR PERSONAL GROWTH: G.R.O.W.T.H

G   **Grow** your internal senses by tuning in consciously to areas in your life which you wish to change and expand; for example, increasing your capacity for developing loving relationships, developing more flexible attitudes, increasing self-confidence, expanding skills and talents, and so on. Write them down if helpful.

R   **Realise** your potential for your future by imagining and planning the steps you might take towards transformation; for example, seek feedback and support from friends; enter a counselling program for clearing out past grievances or unhelpful behaviours; join like-minded groups or personal development seminar programs, both in person and online; begin a new course; and so on.

O   **Open** your mind, body, heart and spirit, as this is helpful for cultivating attitudes that welcome change. This can be achieved by varied means including allowing time for quiet reflection or meditation to rest the mind and open the heart to experience emotional release when needed; nurturing the physical body with healthy vital liquids and foods; refreshing the spirit by listening to music; connecting with art; and communing with natural elements like trees, water and breezes, perhaps even in the home garden or local park. Stand barefoot on the earth which scientists tell us emits electrons helpful for the body's energy renewal.

W   **Wonder** and be curious about other people's ideas, not only through deep discussions with friends but through seeking the knowledge and wisdom of all the great authors and speakers who have inspired so many people on their personal development journey. Read any of the books or watch webinars of the teachings of Wayne Dyer, Louise Hay, Deepak Chopra, Eckhart Tolle, Joe Dispenza — just a very few of the eminent figures in this space. Undertake seminars and courses such as those offered by Brandon Bays and her husband Kevin

Billett. Search for the understandings of the eastern gurus and philosophers as well since great wisdom and truth emanates from their sense of the attitudes and energies that enrich our life and bring new personal insights.

T **Think** outside the box as often as possible and challenge yourself to deliberately change the routine way of life to increase excitement and develop a sense of adventure. Observe and celebrate the best parts of yourself, giving credit for the achievements of your life so far; plan a new strategy to add elements you may find more fulfilling, such as doing something you have always wanted to do; and jump out of your comfort zone often, so that you dance and sing your life into delight.

H **Help** yourself to grow emotionally by fully engaging both with the painful emotions of life as well as the pleasurable experiences. We know that highs and lows may mean long stretches of sadness and disappointment in life, but by consciously seeking insights from those low times, we can gain a deeper understanding of ourselves. This then encourages us to expand our thinking about what creates a meaningful life, as well as opening us to greater gratitude and arousing a vast range of emotional responses which improve our interactions with the world.

NOTE: It is worth remembering that personal growth can be severely restricted by behaviours that sabotage us and cause self-destruction. Drugs and alcohol mask emotions rather than allowing their free and healthy expression. Procrastination is a way of avoiding change. Extreme self-criticism, blaming ourselves and others, and making ourselves victims of life will turn us away from many possibilities for lasting personal growth and fulfilment in life.

12

H. Heartfulness Quotient

HOW OPEN-HEARTED ARE YOU?

An Angel in India

At the age of 11, a small boy with a huge, loving heart, knew it was his destiny to save the unloved children of India. A visit from Singapore, where he grew up, to his father's village in India, shocked this small boy to his heart when he realised that there were hundreds of homeless and abandoned children all through the country.

So many young children were dying with no loving family and no future! The tragedy of this struck young Ravi as if he had a brick weighing down his own heart. He returned to Singapore with a deep desire to come back to India as an adult and save as many children as possible.

He studied Engineering, found a good job and saved all his money in order to pay for the setting up of a home for the poor and abandoned children. He dedicated all his own money and every ounce of his energy to creating 'homes' for children who needed to be rescued from the dangers of living on railway stations and in rubbish dumps. They were vulnerable to bad influences, prostitution, exploitation and illness. Ravi's aim was to provide for their material and social needs as well as to give them an education.

Over the thirty years since Ravi began his work, he has created five homes, each with schools, both in large cities and in country areas of India. He has provided a loving and safe family environment for over 3,000 children, many of whom have studied for university degrees and obtained good jobs. The children think of him as a loving father, for he has dedicated his life to their welfare and been a champion for their future potential.

Whether abandoned, disabled, sick, injured or depressed, all children are welcome. Ravi's huge generous heart is there for them. He always finds a way to help by trusting that The Universe will somehow provide as needed. A visit to one of Ravi's homes named Apna Ghar (Our Home) is a delight and an inspiration, for the children are filled with positivity and excitement as they share their lives together as brothers and sisters.

So many children continue to be saved and encouraged to thrive.

Ravi even gave up opportunities for marriage and children of his own because any potential relationships were unable to survive the life of dedication required for his mission in life. Ravi is no ordinary human, although he is truly a man for all people. His warmth and extraordinary dedication to helping youngsters who would most certainly have struggled to survive places him in the category of a modern-day angel and similar to the likes of the saint, Mother Teresa. It was his huge capacity for Heartfulness that motivated Ravi to give up his comfortable, successful life in Singapore for his greater purpose of saving some of the poorest children on Earth.

HEARTFULNESS QUOTIENT

The capacity for generosity and loving-kindness to others: our capacity to show Love

Love is the most powerful of all emotions. We may be acutely disturbed by the power of hatred and revenge, for these are overwhelming feelings, but it is love that transforms and heals the human heart. Therefore, opening our heartfulness, our capacity for love, is of utmost importance and priority for our well-being.

It is no wonder that films, songs, great art and books about love have dominated our culture; after all, this is the most highly-sought experience — to be in love. Author and speaker Leo Buscaglia once said, 'You can love everybody you meet and never run out of your capacity to love. It is an infinite resource.' It is good to remember this when we meet people in our life, for showing loving-kindness to others spreads goodness, positive energy and joy to ourselves and those with whom we interact.

Psycho-neurologist Paul Pearsall's research book, *The Heart's Code: Tapping the Wisdom and Power of Our Heart Energy*, reveals the 'intelligence' of the heart through experiences of heart transplant and cancer patients. In the past, it was believed that only the brain was the centre of thinking, but there is much evidence now to suggest that the heart is more than just a 'pump' for the body; it has cellular connections that create powerful energies that can inform the body of its well-being and feelings at the deepest level. While we know that the heart does not have the number of neurons or capacity to 'think' like the brain, it does 'communicate' to the brain and body in such a way that we sense emotions as though they come from the heart. Joe Dispenza's insightful book, Becoming Supernatural, devotes a chapter to 'Heart Intelligence', reminding us that the ancients 'believed the heart, rather than the brain, was the centre of life and the source of human wisdom'. Thus, all the expressions relating to the heart and feelings are familiar and somehow believable. We understand the feeling of broken-heartedness; of a stressed beating heart when in an anxiety state; and somehow, we have all felt that it is our heart that seeks to connect us deeply to the emotional aspects of ourselves. Therefore, when a personal challenge confronts us, we are often advised to 'follow our heart', which is a natural and fulfilling strategy to remember. Ravi's story above is exemplary of a life lived fully from trusting his heart to show him the way to change the lives of thousands of poor Indian children.

When our Heartfulness Quotient is low, we can increase it by consciously raising our awareness of the emotional guidance system of our heart

SWITCH STRATEGIES FOR HEARTFULNESS: C.A.R.E.

C **Consciously bring awareness to the centres of the heart and the mind and know which is guiding your life at different times.** There are moments when we feel conflicted between what we THINK we should do (our mind informing us) and what we FEEL we wish to do (our heart informing us).

We often feel our mind is more powerful because it has the added force of judgement and can 'shout' many 'should' phrases at us: 'You should be more careful!' or 'You shouldn't do that!'. Too much 'shoulding' can lead to guilt and misery, as it is often very destructive to ourselves and our lives. Our mind often plays policeman, checking up on us constantly and telling us when we are wrong, worthless or failing. The mind judgement of 'Should' may be helpful in dangerous situations (e.g. 'I should not go into the surf now because it's dangerous!'), but if it begins to dominate our everyday thinking ('I *should/should not* do this or that'), we may find our heart loses its voice and becomes a mere 'whisper' which we seldom hear. There are very important moments when our heart speaks like an internal guidance system, and we need to listen for our health and well-being. It tells us we are kind, loving and capable; it encourages us. To hear the yearning of the heart, it helps to be in a place of peacefulness and calm and to listen to its wisdom, for there is great power in its knowing. Author and actor, Henry Winkler, reflected: 'The mind only knows some things. Your inner voice, your instinct (or heart), knows everything.'

A   **Attract loving energy into your life and cultivate a joyful heart.** We all know what brings us joy and delight, so we will be better off doing more of the wonderful, enriching pursuits. There is always an exchange of energy between people when in close connection. Loving energy attracts, while critical, rejecting energy repels people. Animals know this instinctively and react to loving energy.

R   **Reach out with a generous, giving heart and do kind things to others.** Showing care and concern for people doesn't cost us but returns goodness in abundance. Spread loving warm words like rose petals in your path — not criticism, which is like stones you must walk on to get to others.

E   **Express love for self and others often as it is the most abundant, wonderful feeling – far more satisfying in life than material abundance.** Cultivating our heartfulness brings all kinds of love into our lives.

13

I. Intuition Quotient

HOW STRONG IS YOUR INTUITION?

Saved by Intuition

When I was a young woman of 22, I set off to see the world starting in London. If not for following my intuition, I may have never come home.

One evening, after a concert, I was waiting for a taxi to take me from Central London to a suburb about 40 minutes away when a couple asked if they could share a taxi ride to North London. At first, I felt a little uncertain but agreed. Since they were two and I was one person, it seemed logical to have them in the back and me in the front with the driver.

What a mistake! They got to their destination in 15 minutes and got out, leaving me alone with the driver. The doors were locked.

Very soon after, the driver began to make lewd comments, suggesting he and I were a good 'match'. Being a foreigner, he assumed rightly that I did not know my way around this huge city and as his vulgar comments increased, I tried to ignore them and simply kept my remarks to a minimum; but I felt very uneasy.

The situation became highly disturbing when I realised we were driving way into the country and nowhere near the place I was staying. He feigned being 'lost' and said he did not know where to go to get me 'home'. I sat quietly, looking straight ahead, but a silent panic rose within me when he slyly remarked, 'This is a forest we are in, and we know what happened when the Big Bad Wolf had Red Riding Hood in the forest!' I sensed he was definitely trying to scare me and with nothing but farmhouses surrounding us on one side and a forest on the other, I began to imagine I might be murdered here.

I even contemplated my body being in the forest and never found by my grieving family back in Australia. My mind ran amok, but I listened to my gut feeling — my intuition — which guided me not to show him my fear as I felt he was enjoying trying to make me afraid.

My mind was creating the worst-case scenario knowing the driver had the most powerful position as he sped through the countryside to who knows where.

But my intuition told me to hide my fear and 'take back control' of the situation.

I suddenly saw a sign to a town, and I directed him to turn the car and go to the town. He kept arguing that 'That is not where you want to go', but I ignored him and firmly insisted he turn left then drive to the town centre. I continued to direct him as if I expected him to follow my instructions and when I found a couple of places with lights still on late that night, I ordered him to stop and unlock the car door. He did so, to my surprise, and I leapt out of the car in a flash, rushing into a building with people inside. I was able to escape and get help while he drove off into the night.

I truly believe that even though I didn't act on my instinct to not get into the front seat, listening to my intuition to keep calm and take control perhaps deterred a potentially dangerous man.

INTUITION QUOTIENT

The extent to which we have a tendency to trust our gut feeling about people and situations

Intuition is the ability that all of us have to instinctively sense people and situations without intellectual reasoning. Sometimes, we just 'get a feeling' about someone or something, especially when the situation suggests danger. It is most often activated when things do not seem 'right' as it triggers our body's innate warning system and guides us. This is the basis of our 'stranger danger' programs with children that involves teaching our youngsters to be aware that 'if a situation makes them uncomfortable inside', they should move away and tell an adult. It can be a powerful sense for all of us to develop for our safety and well-being, but it is often viewed with scepticism by intellectual rationalists.

We all understand and activate our senses of taste, touch, sight, smell and hearing, fully understanding how these provide tangible information about our world. Sometimes, it is simply a feeling, a memory, or impression gained through symbolic images that activates our intuition, our sixth sense, as it is sometimes called. Nearly all of us have experienced the sense of déjà vu — of having been somewhere new before or having previously known someone we have just met — and many of us have had encounters with unusual connecting events like thinking of someone just before they ring us. Some people say coincidence is responsible for linked unusual experiences; others believe our intuition tunes in to certain frequencies and connects with patterns of events across the Universe. Synchronicities are common, but sometimes, we may have unusual experiences that baffle or surprise us. If we accept that intuition can assist us to know our heart's desires more deeply, then we can see value in increasing our intuitive abilities.

*When our Intuition Quotient is low
and we wish to increase it, we can apply some
strategies to improve it*

SWITCH STRATEGIES TO INCREASE INTUITION: GO I.N.S.I.D.E

I **Intuition is a sense of inner knowing that we all have. Become aware of this sense that is often accompanied by intense feelings,** for example, when we sense the unhappiness of others despite their outer positive face and we feel an underlying sadness; or when we feel afraid, even anxiously sick in the stomach, for an unknown reason. These are indicators of intuitive feelings. Keep a diary of these instances.

N **Nature has a powerful effect in heightening our senses.** If we walk in nature with activated senses, we will have a different experience from passive interaction. Nature has a power 'to come to us' through the winds, sun and scents, but Tristan Gooley, in *How to Read Nature*, believes that by 'tuning in to what our eyes, ears, nose and face are trying to tell us about the sky (and nature), we open up half of a new world'. Be in nature and fully engage. I used to come home from a day's work during summer, go into my yard and lie on my back on the grass looking up at the sky with clouds wisping and floating above me. It used to completely open my heart and refresh my mind. Tune in to feelings and ideas you receive in nature and expand them with the question: 'What messages are coming to me about my life?'

S **Silence has magic if we can appreciate it. It is valuable to make time for silent contemplation in order to give our inner voice space to be heard**. Julia Baird's book, *Phosphorescence*, devotes a whole chapter to silence, reminding us that times of quiet are rare in such a frenzied and technological world. Allow small spaces in each day to slip out of busyness into peacefulness even for a few minutes, when possible. Close your eyes and breathe deeply as you ask yourself, 'What am I feeling now?' Get in touch with that inner still small voice.

I **Interpret synchronicities and coincidences in a fun way to increase your awareness of possible intuitive**

understandings. There is no right or wrong answer when our internal knowing system activates: it is there to add a new dimension to our senses, for it is our sixth sense which can only be powerful if we believe it to be. Many people do not wish to hear or believe in their intuitive voice for various reasons. This is perfectly acceptable for they may feel they do not need the insight that it may bring. Often, the highly scientific mind will reject what is not easily provable, but quantum physics is revealing many previously unbelievable mysteries of the invisible world of energy.

D **Dreams are a great source of information for unveiling our subconscious thoughts and feelings.** Many famous researchers have studied the phenomena relating to dreams, not the least of whom was the psychologist Carl Jung. While the interpretation of dreams is quite an art, it is worth thinking about the themes that recur in our dreams for these can give insights into our inner world. One of my students used to have a recurring dream of being trapped in a locked room and unable to get to the examination centre. When I asked what he felt and what he thought on waking, he said he felt anxious about missing the exam. This is just a simple example of how a dream might echo some inner, quite normal, insecurities that do not seem as obvious on the surface. Recording our dreams and the feelings they elicit is often helpful for igniting more intuitive experiences.

E **Experiences and questions which challenge us can be explored through sending out intentions to the Universal energy** with the expectation of receiving some signs or thoughts and feelings that bring a 'knowing' of what to do. Meditation is a very powerful way of sensing intuitive answers. After our youngest brother, Mark, died quite young, three out of four of his siblings began to find five-cent pieces lying in plain sight but in unusual places. We all felt the weirdness of instances like sweeping the floor and immediately finding one of these coins in the middle of the area just swept. Sometimes, I would talk about my brother and a five-cent coin would drop out of nowhere and land in front of me. Friends who witnessed this strange phenomenon said they could not believe it until the proof came directly for them to see. Each of us came to intuitively believe that Mark's energy was sending a sign and connecting with us still. Believe it or not!

14

J. Joy Quotient

HOW DO YOU SEEK AND OPEN YOURSELF TO JOY?

Moonlight Magic

In the remote Australian outback, a secret and beautiful salt lake was the setting for one of the most joyful experiences of my life. I had never seen such a huge expanse of salty whiteness. It looked like a shimmering lake, but it was firm enough to walk on.

Our camp for the night was set up among twisty, shrubby trees on the pale sandy shore, and there was not another human anywhere in this amazing wilderness.

But after dark, the magic began!

When dinner was done, my love and I sat still, a glass of wine in hand, and waited for the gentle darkness to surround us, to seep into our souls. We closed our eyes in meditation, aware only of peaceful silence but not expecting the vision that was to come. When our eyes opened, an incredible, huge, full moon had risen on the horizon.

It was breathtakingly beautiful but made more spectacular by the sparkling light magnified across the gleaming crystalline lake! It was an 'Oh My God!' moment in life.

A spontaneous burst of joy arose from my heart, and I began to sing into the silence. Remote and mystical as it was, it seemed so natural to slip out of our clothes and step onto the moonlight pathway streaming across the lake. We sang and danced, rapt in the moment, with our bare feet hugging the salty surface.

Everyone should find such unforgettable moments of pure joy in life!

JOY QUOTIENT

The openness to seek joyful experiences in life

Joy is an emotion of great delight and elation caused by something good that creates an immensely enriching experience. While happiness is pleasing and satisfying, it is more of a state of being. Joy is a feeling often aroused within a state of happiness and seems to appear with sudden intensity. We sometimes equate joy with ecstasy as it seems like a blissful, often temporary, feeling that we all look to experience. When we danced in the moonlight that night, it was a temporary moment of joy, but wonderful enough to last a lifetime. This is what joy can do: give us moments we will never forget!

To experience joy, we must be open to sense every moment of possibility for it and seek it in every simple place it may be waiting for us. Sometimes, joy is elusive, and we have to create it by placing ourselves in its pathway and grabbing it as often as possible. There are many dozens of quotations on joy to be googled, but all indicate that joy is found within us since the openness to find joy, even in ordinary moments, is a blessing.

My counselling office was always decorated with colourful banners and sayings to remind me and my fellow humans that there is great power in elevating our thoughts and feelings through visual and verbal reminders. I remember a senior teacher who came to my office to refer a troubled student for counselling and when I welcomed him into the room, asking him what brought him to me, he looked at my sayings on the walls and scoffed, 'I don't want any of that "happiness" stuff!!'

I could not believe that anyone could be so negative and yet expect to be a major support to young people. I have always unashamedly expressed my positivity openly, and I believe that people who cynically criticise those who seek personal growth through heart-centred practices like speaking personal affirmations and displaying positive visual imagery are, sadly, revealing a degree of hard-heartedness and a closed mind. It is wonderful to live life not only seeking joy in beautiful things like nature, art, music and friendship but to go looking under rocks and broken dreams for little specks of joy that can be brought to light and savoured.

When our Joy Quotient is low and we wish to raise it, there are strategies that help us live more joyfully

SWITCH STRATEGIES TO ELEVATE JOYFULNESS: S.E.E.K J.O.Y

S **Sensitize** yourself to feeling and seeking joy as often as possible and in as many ways as possible. Find activities that bring joy: artistic and creative pursuits, time with animals, celebrations for even the smallest thing, gardening and growing vegetables and flowers, hanging out with friends and family, playing and watching sports, watching films and plays, baking and cooking wonderful foods, and so many more experiences.

E **Energise** and raise your emotional level when feeling flat by using mental, physical and emotional strategies. Think yourself into taking action which will bring happier, joyful feelings. For example, use self-talk to decide to feel joyful: 'I am not going to sit here feeling tired and flat, I'm going to bring myself to joy by going for a walk and noticing flowers and trees and feeling the wind on my face or the sunshine on my skin.' The simple act of choosing music to move us emotionally, or playing music for dancing, can energise our body and soul. There are many things that each of us can do to consciously raise our joy each day.

E **Experience** life in all its ups and downs. It is often said that we experience joy more fully if we have known great pain. Joy is more joyful if we have suffered deeply.

I remember so vividly how a very dear friend going through a terrible loss for many months woke up one day and shouted out into the air: 'I have suffered enough! I have learned a few things and now I'm looking for joy in my life!' If we choose to live in The Land of Suffering for too long, we may generate and attract sad and heavy energy and forget how to seek joy altogether.

K **Know** what brings joy into your life and consciously choose to do more of those things. Seek people who make you feel joyful: these are people who have attitudes of fun and positivity. Be with those who make you laugh when you are down and keep connected to the people you need to hug. Always hug often. There is research that reveals how 20 seconds of hugging is enough to elevate our feelings. Hug pets also for they understand joy in the simplest way. As Khalil Gibran reminds us in *The Prophet*, 'forget not that the earth delights to feel your bare feet and the winds long to play with your hair'.

J **Join** in with anything that promises to celebrate life's beauty and wonder. Celebrate as often as possible, not just on special occasions. Make up reasons to celebrate! Every person who attends or organises Friday afternoon drinks invites pleasure and celebration into their week. Each time we choose joy by curling up with a book or cuddling up to watch a film alone or with others, we show our heart that we are taking care of it by nurturing it with happy experiences. Our heart and our soul NEED joy to survive. There is a particular heart syndrome called 'Takotsubo cardiomyopathy' (TCM) which is specifically related to broken-heartedness. Our whole being thrives on joy and can even die without it!

O **Own** your optimism and positivity in the face of cynics and naysayers. Hang out positive affirmation banners and place sayings and words around your environment if they help remind you to focus on joyful feelings. We have the word LOVE stuck on the wall opposite our bed so that, each morning, we wake to the reminder that life is more meaningful if we remember to bring love to life each day. If this is not your way, that is fine too. But be wary of spending too much time around people who bring you down, not through sadness necessarily because we need to be there for our friends no matter what, but through negativity, for which we do not need to put out the welcome mat!

Y **Yellow** is the colour of Sunshine. Bring it into your life, along with all the other spectacular colours of the rainbow. Never forget to embrace the positive joy we can feel through colourful clothes, furnishings and house design. Let the sunshine in with streaming light through windows and by standing in its healing rays. And that goes for the magic of the moonlight as well, for it is pure inspiration and an invitation to bathe in joy.

15

K. Knowledge Quotient

HOW WELL DO YOU SEEK AND FIND KNOWLEDGE?

Please Share With the Class!

Melinda was a student to whom I taught English during my first years as a young teacher. I have never forgotten her attitude to learning because her mind was expanded constantly through avid reading. These days, a 'Melinda-like student' would be searching for information on the internet. Then, it was mostly books as knowledge source.

Melinda was passionate about literature and drama. When we studied Dylan Thomas's poetry and Oscar Wilde's plays, she went to the library (since there was no internet and Google in those days) and researched their lives and works in order to fully understand what inspired the literature they created.

So knowledgeable did she become about them that I invited her to give a class now and then to add her knowledge and passion to the energy and learning for the rest of her classmates and me. I was a teacher on a learning journey who could recognise that some students are brilliant, and since I was only a few years older than her at the time, I believed her passion was a wonderful example to others.

It is not surprising that, with her intellect, she could have studied any course, but she chose to become an English teacher. No doubt, she still continues to pass on her passion to generations of young people.

KNOWLEDGE QUOTIENT

The level of curiosity for knowledge in general or in particular

While Knowledge is the facts, skills and information that we acquire through education and experience, our current digital age has created both new exciting avenues for learning as well as challenges in learning as a result of the availability of information that has grown exponentially. Never before has information been so easily acquired; however, the huge problem of reliability of sources has led to the difficulty of sorting through information that is factually correct and that which is either simply an opinion or 'fake news'.

At the touch of a finger on our phones nowadays, we can find out the answer to almost anything we wish to know.

Everyone seeks knowledge at times — whether for career development, medical information, or simply to research the best product on the market prior to purchase. This ready availability of knowledge at our fingertips is an amazingly valuable resource; however, with social media and internet marketing pop-ups hugely dominant in so many of our lives, it has become difficult to know whether our information is from reliable sources.

Most people find the shortcut of getting news online and from social media much easier and therefore, even though much information is simply opinion that has no specified origin, it is often taken as truth and shared with others again and again. Sometimes, we hear people say, 'I don't need to read books, watch the news and current affairs or learn from experts.' It has even been suggested that opinion, and especially a personal view of an issue, is all that we need. Some people have scant knowledge of world and societal issues and yet they offer up personal perceptions as opinions with full confidence that they are totally valid, whether or not they are based on genuine evidence.

Opinions make positive contributions to any discussion on issues, but these must also reveal awareness of factual information. The reason for the power of the 'Black Lives Matter' anti-racist demonstrations in many parts of the world was the fact that clear video footage of police violence plus facts about the number of deaths at the hands of police provided a firm factual basis for opinions to be valid.

Why is increasing and enhancing our knowledge important? It is because it connects us to so many other important aspects of our lives. If we want to find our passion or enhance it, we need to know as much about it as possible through seeking information. If we wish to increase our career and life skills, we can look to experts as vast sources of knowledge. For personal development, there is much information and so many ideas to be discovered.

When my former student, Melinda, independently followed her curious mind to discover more knowledge of the literature she was studying, she learned far more than her school classes could provide, and it led to a lifelong passion that created her career direction and changed her life. Expanding our knowledge is a lifelong project that has the capacity to enhance and transform our lives in ways we may never imagine until, one day, something arises that reveals how important it is for us to acquire a particular gem of knowledge. The more knowledgeable we are, the more interesting is our conversation, and the more meaningful is the sharing with people we meet on our life journey.

When our Knowledge Quotient is in need of a boost, there are helpful strategies to increase our capacity to learn and gain knowledge

SWITCH STRATEGIES FOR KNOWLEDGE: K.N.O.W.

K   **Knowledge** is acquired both passively through hearing information and actively through seeking it. A very immediate and excellent source of information to add to our knowledge base is, of course, Google. It is part of our life now to google almost anything every day: 'What time is the next train?' or 'Who was the inventor who created the light bulb?' and so on, endlessly. I know someone who has conversations with people and, any time anyone raises a question worth knowing, he googles on the spot and shares it if helpful for the question. He is an avid seeker of knowledge and has a sense of 'active immediacy' — always ready to find out — as he travels through life. We just always need to check the sources of the information to make sure they are reliably correct. And never forget how wonderful it can be to curl up with a book and read!

N   **New** information needs a system for remembering what is needed and forgetting what is useless.

- Write down the things you wish to remember in a little notebook that you carry within reach — bag or car or pocket.

- Make up a **mnemonic** (meaning memory) like the one in this section of this book where the word **KNOW** becomes a reminder of the information to remember. Alternatively, make another form of mnemonic called an **acrostic** in which the first letter of each word in a memory list is made into a sentence such as Every Good Boy Deserves Fruit, where EGBDF are the names of the notes in the treble clef in music notation.

- Draw stick-figure pictures and diagrams, and use colours as visual reminders for information to remember.

O   **Outsource** the acquisition of information you need by finding experts who can help to give you information or direct you to a better expert. Ask others what they know, who they know and where you can go for the best knowledge available in whatever field you are researching. For a small fee, you can even employ an online company like Freelancer.com to find experts all over the world or people who will research and write up information as needed.

W **Wonder** about everything and be curious for knowledge and understanding about the world. Make the effort to find out more about everything that interests you. A knowledgeable person is greatly admired and respected as well as being interesting to talk to and share time with in any social setting.

16

L. Laughter Quotient

CAN YOU LAUGH EASILY AND LIGHTEN UP FOR RELAXATION?

Get Your Suits Out, Boys!

It seems that there could be nothing worse than receiving the news that you are dying.

Certainly, no one expects joking about it. But my younger brother, Mark, was 42 when he was told to get his 'affairs in order'. That's a pathetic euphemism for "you're dying"! He rang me first. 'I've got kidney cancer. I'm screwed!' He then rang all his mates with his news and announced: 'You'd better get your suit out ready for my funeral!'

In a short number of weeks, he was gravely ill, and the day the doctor told him it was time for palliative care, he joked with the doctor, 'Isn't it time you call House?' referring to the television series of the same name. House always seemed to find a way of saving his patients, and Mark's joke in the face of personal disaster was incredible to us. At his funeral, his best friend remembered that 'Mark was the funniest man I've ever met, yet he never told a joke. He just had a way of seeing the funny side of life, no matter what was happening.'

LAUGHTER QUOTIENT

The ability to see the humorous side of life

Laughter is the emotion of release, and it simply feels good to laugh!

Everyone loves the positive feelings we receive from this natural reaction. We not only laugh when something is funny, but sometimes, when anxiety is great, we also laugh nervously. This allows us to relax in a tense situation. There is also a social purpose in laughter. The author of *Humor and Laughter: An Anthropological Approach* and cultural anthropologist Mahadev Apte believes that laughing results in greater bonding within a group. There is a feedback loop of bonding-laughter-more bonding which makes laughter contagious.

When Mark, above, joked about getting the suits out for his funeral, it seemed to have had two purposes: firstly, to help his friends cope better with the bad news and secondly, to downplay the tragedy for Mark himself. This was his unique way of not burdening others with his calamity. Laughter can be a coping mechanism in dramatic or stressful circumstances.

In my twenties, as my friends and I were exploring life as young adults, I vividly remember a close friend arriving often late at night, tearful and distressed about the latest issue with a particular boyfriend, and when I opened the door, she would always simultaneously cry and laugh with the words, 'Life's a bugger!' We would both joke about her bad luck before unpacking her latest grief at the situation but somehow laughing at herself for getting into that circumstance. The positive thing about this was that she had a consciousness of her own part in creating her life and could see that her difficulties were just as much the result of her choice of 'boyfriend type' as they were the actions of the man. Her laughter at the absurdity of life for her, helped her to reflect on her behaviour and make changes to her reactions. She also chose to 'laugh at life' rather than be a victim of the men who caused her such pain.

The best reason to develop a good sense of humour and laugh often is simply because it feels good, and it helps improve our well-being. Our world has become so full of dark themes of violence, bad news, disaster stories and negativity, that our films and social media are a conduit for exposure to tragedy, so immediately as they happen, it can be depressing. Rates of depression and suicide are unbelievably high, especially in fortunate first world countries. Fortunately, social media also provides avenues for quick access to humour, and this is a positive side of freely available mediums.

> *When our Laughter Quotient needs a lift, we can take action to increase our ability to see the lighter side of life*

SWITCH STRATEGIES FOR LAUGHTER: F.U.N.

F **Fun** is wonderful for everyone! Look for times and places to have fun, laugh and play, then do it often. Laughing while we do something silly is a means of escape from the serious side of life; laughing at ourselves is a healthy way of disabling 'victimhood'; and spending time with humorous people helps us refresh and lower stress. Become consciously aware of how often in a day you laugh, and if the environment is not conducive to laughter, allow for short bursts of YouTube, watching people and animals doing silly things. I'm sure that the reason people enjoy becoming tipsy with wine is that inhibitions are lowered, and we enjoy laughing more easily. Never underestimate the power of laughing. Where there is Laughter, we often also find Joy, so switch on to laugh every day and often.

U **Upsides** can be found in so many situations and seeking the funny side of serious situations is helpful. In counselling, we frequently use 'reframing' as a good technique to switch our minds out of negative situations with humour often helping to trigger this change. For example, 'This happened, but it could have been worse!' Play with that old joke that has been around for decades: Do you want the good news or bad news? The bad news is that I lost my wallet, but the good news is I found it. The bad news is that money was stolen from it, but the good news is that it was only a small amount of cash, and so on.

N **Natural** laughter is to be welcomed without embarrassment and with a sense of freedom, however, there are many popular laughing workshops that have sprung up all over the world and they are fun and energising. The experience of developing techniques for getting laughter activated can make us feel self-conscious, but inhibitions dissolve in company with people all laughing together. It's worth trying if you feel you have lost your capacity for laughter. Another inspiration for laughter is, of course, the comedy we experience from films and YouTube clips. There are stories of famous people who have faced death and extended their lives by continuously watching funny films and laughing for hours.

17

M. Mindfulness Quotient

HOW AWARE ARE YOU OF LIVING IN THE NOW?

How will I ever get there?

Anthony was only fourteen, but the weight of the world was on his shoulders. He was constantly worried about the future. How would he get through school? How would he pass the end-of-year exams? What would happen if he failed the test next week?

So stressed was he about what might happen in the circumstances in which he might find himself next week, next year, or in five years when school would be over, that he could not function in the present. Anticipating future catastrophe every day was making him sick with anxiety and depressed about his life.

He was an extreme case of someone for whom mindfulness was a struggle, for if he took his mind off the future, he feared that he would not make it. His self-talk was also sabotaging him and preventing him from functioning effectively.

It was a mammoth effort to get Anthony through the next five years of secondary school. He would sit in my counselling office in a state of angst many, many times in the coming years. However, he made great improvement with the support of our school and his parents who understood their son's difficulties.

The key to helping him cope was to teach him to focus on the NOW with mindfulness strategies — to realise that the now was a series of stepping stones on a pond. As long as he kept focusing on each step, he could use each of the stones to get him across the pond safely. If he had to traverse a larger lake or river in the future, he could 'make a boat in his mind'. By switching his mind away from dealing with potential future catastrophic possibilities to managing present small difficulties, he could then learn how to cope with life more effectively.

Anthony needed to understand and accept that he did not have to 'swim' over every waterway and risk drowning. He could find his own 'boats'! And they were in his mind!

He learned calming, diversionary techniques, such as stopping a panic reaction by leaving his desk, going out to the garden, breathing in number patterns and focusing on the immediate surroundings in nature. This helped calm his anxiety. With special arrangements to sit apart from others during exams, he was able to complete his education. Nevertheless, it was a long journey. But he made it!

MINDFULNESS QUOTIENT

The process of deliberately bringing our attention to experiences happening in the present moment and accepting them without judgement

It is surprising that few of us have a natural capacity for awareness of the present moment, much less having the inclination to bring conscious attention to our feelings, thoughts, body sensations and environment. Our lives can become so busy as we move from one thing to the next, then the next and so on until each day and week passes without much cognisance of the passing of time. 'Mindfulness' has become a popular concept to express the process and practices of learning to observe ourselves in our present moment without using criticism and judgement about our life or the experiences we encounter. But why is mindfulness of value? Surely life just goes on each day, and we capture the time we have available to do what we must do. We often don't have time to stop and be mindful because we are always moving forward towards the future.

Eckhart Tolle, renowned author of *The Power of Now*, among other thought-provoking books, believes that we need to 'realise that now is all there ever is; there is no past or future except as memory or anticipation in your mind'. How can this be? It seems simple, but of course, it is not because we are complex humans.

Naturally, we all understand that we are living in the present, but many of us do not have a conscious awareness of how we are navigating the moments of our present lives. We may be stuck on events and experiences of the past: remembering wonderful times, trying to obliterate disappointments, regretting actions and choices made, and trying to make sense of tragedies in our lives. We can also become completely goal-focused as we forge ahead to the future, looking for a state of happiness, creating plans for success, and making choices to follow our best pathway in life.

Psychologists and counsellors who listen to the anguish of people have come to realise that most depression is a result of regrets and suffering from the past and that most anxiety is caused by fear of what might happen in the future. It is no wonder that our hearts and minds are drawn away from the present: we have so much depression or anxiety to steal our life's energy! In between this is a present in which we are trying to catch up on unfinished business from the past and propel ourselves into tomorrow.

If we stop and truly think about the present moment, we can understand how powerful it can be to fully experience NOW and all its possibilities. Let us be clear that living in an awareness of NOW does not mean that we justify a life of inaction towards the future or that we 'do whatever we want now' because there is no need to consider what might happen. We do not say, 'All I have is today, so I will eat, sleep and do whatever pleases me!' Rather, we can live our life more mindfully by switching from an automatic life with daily tasks and distractions to increasing awareness of what we are doing and paying attention to the feelings, thoughts and body sensations of the 'experience' of living.

Several cultures have created words for a deliberate

awareness of 'presence' in daily life. For example, in Denmark, 'Hugge'(meaning 'cosy') describes the idea of finding pleasure in simple moments like sitting quietly while savouring a cup of coffee. In Japan, 'Ikigai' describes the idea of finding our purpose and what makes us happy. It is believed that taking life more slowly and deliberately and with greater self-awareness brings contentment and peace which, in turn, allows space for deeper personal reflection and insight.

Mindfulness is empowering because it encourages greater thoughtfulness about our lives. It allows us to decide whether we wish to continue as we are or change what we are doing. It also encourages us not to criticise or judge any of our thoughts and feelings but to accept and understand them.

Most of us have experienced the kind of thinking that leads to worrying. Lying awake in bed worrying about people or things happening in our lives can lead us to get on a 'train of thought' that takes us to the same boring destination — anxiety and discomfort. Mindfulness practice brings our attention to that 'train of thought' and encourages us to choose metaphorically whether to 'stay' on that train (keep worrying) till the end destination, or 'get off' at an earlier station (divert our attention from worry) and go somewhere else. With conscious awareness, we can learn to change our worry behaviours.

When Mindfulness is difficult, it can be helpful to practice some strategies

SWITCH STRATEGIES FOR MINDFULNESS: N.O.W.

N **Now** is the moment to be aware of thoughts, feelings, actions. We can learn to tune in to our immediate state of being and switch to choosing mindfulness practices whenever needed. Leaving a place of high activity or a situation of stress for a short time can release us to focus on peaceful, calm thoughts for even a few minutes. We can all do this often in our lives by finding a quiet, comfortable place to sit indoors or outdoors and focusing on our breathing (especially, regular breathing practice: breathe in deeply counting to 4 – hold for 4 counts – breath out for 4 counts. Repeat several times.).

O **Observation** is a vital aspect of Mindfulness. Noticing small features of everyday life using all our senses and feeling gratitude for them is important for becoming more mindful. The delight of flavours in food, the scent of plants, the colours of nature or paints and everything that makes up our surroundings becomes more noticeable if we observe regularly and appreciate details. It is mindful if we take time, even short bursts, to sit quietly and close our eyes, allowing sounds and scents to waft around us, receiving thoughts and images but letting them drift away rather than settle with us. If disturbing thoughts or images come to us, we can stop that train of thought by consciously breaking the thought and turning our attention elsewhere (Imagine stopping the train at a station and getting out so the thoughts are interrupted).

W Whisper in your own ear as you talk to yourself about your reactions to experiences. If your thoughts are creating anxiety rather than inviting them to expand, deflect them with powerful self-talk which switches off the negative anxious energy and switches on positive thoughts and supportive feelings. Shakespeare's character, Hamlet, spoke truth when he noted, 'Nothing is good or bad but thinking makes it so'. And the famous therapist Albert Ellis created Rational Emotive Therapy based on this same concept that how we think about an event or experience determines our reaction. If we see the darkest elements of a situation, we may draw ourselves into despair, but if we can switch our thinking to another more helpful view, we can change our emotional reaction. This is not always easy or possible in tragic situations; but with Anthony, in the situation above, his thinking was always about the worst-case scenario and panic would follow. By teaching him to be more mindful of his thoughts and feelings, and to distract himself physically, he was able to shift his emotions and cope much more frequently.

18

N. Neutrality Quotient

HOW WELL CAN YOU CONTROL AND REGULATE EMOTIONS WHEN NEEDED?

Rage and Violence

The boys of G M School in the East of London in the 70s were out of control — completely violent and deeply shocking for me as a young teacher on a working holiday.

I was paid extra money for the perceived 'danger' of working there and I took it on as a challenge. It was an experience which I will never forget from then until forever.

These adolescent boys were full of rage for their life situations and their school. They were mostly poor, disadvantaged kids and I counted groups of boys from twelve different nationalities in this school community. Each day, as I passed through the gate, I would witness physical and verbal altercations all over the playground. In the classrooms, minor scuffles were continually breaking out between various racial factions. Some students were continually 'bashed up' by others, and the boys and male teachers seemed to accept a culture of verbal and physical abuse.

From the first day, I was advised not to try and teach them, just to contain them within the class for 40 minutes at a time. The boys would not listen, nor would they stop swearing and shouting at teachers and each other. There were not even any exercise books, pens or reading books in classrooms because they had been continuously stolen or destroyed.

The staff, all men except for me and one other female teacher of drama, had become just as unruly as the boys and frequently modelled violence as a means of control. The boys were hit and abused as much by the teachers as by other students. I saw a hugely tall and terrifying teacher slam a small boy's head into his desk, but the principal didn't care because he did it too! No one — neither the boys nor the adults — could step back and find a neutral perspective in the face of strong emotions.

Volcanoes of feelings were erupting every moment of the day.

The whole school community had little understanding of the value of creating peacefulness and respect as an expectation or a goal.

Within my own class groups, I swam against the current in trying to help the boys find a sense of neutrality so that they could refrain from judgement and open themselves to listening to other students. I can't say I was very successful;

there were flashes of quiet insight, mostly through reading books to them aloud and insisting they take turns to share their thoughts. But, six months later, with all the misogynistic teachers calling me a crazy idealist, I decided my battle was over. But here, I learned the value of taking a position of Neutrality when chaos was exploding.

NEUTRALITY QUOTIENT

The ability to move into a neutral emotional position when high emotions are destructive to self or others

Neutrality is a state or position of impartiality that allows us to step back from strong, often uncontrollable emotions, into a calmer space in order to allow for a lessening of the intensity of a situation.

Most of us are quite capable of regulating our emotions in everyday situations; however, sometimes our emotional response can be extreme to the extent that we can lash out verbally and/or physically resulting in great hurt and pain for others.

Every teacher would be able to make vast lists of students, particularly adolescent boys, who have had difficulty regulating their anger responses and who have caused disruption in the classroom. Many students can experience angry outbursts of behaviour such as throwing objects, lashing out at others, and threatening violence to themselves. Teachers have always had to help students to calm themselves into neutrality so that they could speak about their feelings more openly and respectfully.

In Mental Health circles, this behaviour is known as Emotional Dysregulation (ED) because emotional responses do not lie within the accepted range of emotive responses. Of course, ED is often associated with psychological and medical disorders. Both terrifying and devastating is the situation of violence within an individual, which escalates into mass murder, particularly seen in school shootings which the US experiences all too often. For five years, I worked as a Family Therapist in a school for emotionally disturbed children, most of whom experienced emotional dysregulation, and each one needed to have specific interventions to create opportunities for developing a state of calm neutrality.

Developing strategies for finding our state of Neutrality is valuable for us all for times when we are emotionally stressed beyond reason. That is not to suggest that neutrality is needed when a person expresses grief and anger. Everyone knows how relieving it is to shout, scream or cry into the wind or from the height of a mountain. This is therapeutic. Angry shouting and violence towards another person are not acceptable under any circumstances and this is why understanding Neutrality is essential.

Another important value in finding our Neutrality space is that it helps us to acquire more patience when we have invested great emotional energy in something we wish to happen, and it is not coming to us easily. Sometimes, we try so hard to achieve something or we wish so badly for something, our intensity drives it further from us.

In the spiritual dimension, we may enlist the Law of Attraction to help fulfil our desires, but sometimes, our version of our dream is different from that of the Universe which has its own plan and timing for our life's dreams. Remaining in the 'Sacred Neutral' helps us to put out the desire and simply wait for its time to come.

When reaching a state of Neutrality is a challenge, practising certain strategies can be helpful

SWITCH STRATEGIES FOR DEVELOPING THE STATE OF NEUTRALITY: C.A.L.M

C **Catch** emotions as they arise and become conscious of the degree of feelings associated with the event or the person concerned. Disrupt the progress of negative, angry, rising emotion by physically leaving the scene and diverting attention elsewhere. This might include using physical exercise as an outlet or simply being outside and walking or running. Let the emotion burn itself out into the atmosphere rather than directing it to self or others. Use imagery which appeals to you personally. For example, imagine filling a helium balloon with the emotion and releasing it into the air to fly or float away. Choose your own imaginary release mechanism.

A **Awareness** of personal triggers is helpful for avoiding situations that are disturbing. This is a vital step in understanding how to get to Neutrality more quickly. Of course, there are some people (especially narcissists and gaslighters) who use strong emotions to intimidate others, and there is little motivation to change into a position of Neutrality. It is important, in the case of repeated violent behaviours, that everyone is safe, therefore, if necessary, **seek immediate help** from legal or health professionals. This should be **priority one** in the circumstance. With violent family members who are usually rational and who do not have a mental illness, practising certain steps may help. When mental illness is present with violence, always seek medical support.

L **Learn** positive steps to switch into Neutrality:

- Realise the strong emotion and beware of its intensity on a scale of 1 – 10. If past five, it's time to take the next step.

- Exit the scene and go to a safe, calm place.

- Breathe deeply and find something enjoyable to do to release the tension and relax.

- Connect with someone who understands and can help you talk it through calmly and quietly.

M **Meditate** if this is a practice with which you are familiar. The stillness of meditation practice is calming and provides an excellent way of lowering the intensity of emotions. If you have not learned to meditate, there are many apps and webinars that can help you to learn.

19

O. Optimism Quotient

HOW EASILY DO YOU CULTIVATE AN OPTIMISTIC APPROACH TO LIFE?

No reason to be optimistic...

How do the most 'unfortunate' people in the world keep smiling?

The people in India known as the 'untouchables' — the lowest rung in society — sleep under plastic tarpaulin lean-tos or in the open air, and many spend their days rag picking as they search among the rubbish for anything saleable. Anything to gather a few rupees for their next meal.

On a visit I made to a huge Indian city to see where help could be given to orphaned children, I was humbled by a visit to meet the local 'ragpickers'. Although shocked to find humans living under such intolerable conditions, especially in horrendous hot weather, I was touched by their gesture of finding a broken plastic chair for me to sit on while I talked to them through a friend as the interpreter.

There was no complaining about their lives and no miserable faces, despite tragic human circumstances. In fact, the children were smiling happily and coming forward to show me simple little items they had found — a hairpin, a broken toy, an opened chocolate bar. The group of women, mostly living there with the children, had no husbands to support them, but they formed a supportive community that seemed to provide some security from the danger of possible attack. They all smiled and were keen to meet me — yet none of them looked for a handout of money. I felt that optimism for life was present here among the slums, and it changed me forever to see how little expectation they had of life beyond survival. We Westerners, many of whom enjoy a good quality of life, have much to learn about appreciating our circumstances.

Never would I have expected to go into the rubbish dumps of India and find optimism on the faces of people on the lowest rung of society. But optimism was here! Nor would I expect optimism from someone who was desperate for work yet had no luck after applying month-after-month to 114 jobs. Yet there was also optimism here too! Then, there was a friend who had a run of disabling illnesses which caused her to need a walking apparatus for several years who never asked, 'Why me?' but simply thought 'Why not me?' as she waited for the operation. Here also, was optimism in the face of pain.

In all these circumstances — extreme poverty, a huge disappointment, and severe pain — there were people whose optimism remained strong enough to keep them living positively no matter what happened in their lives.

OPTIMISM QUOTIENT

The degree to which we view the future as full of hope and with possibility for success

Optimism is to be treasured. If we can approach life as if the glass is half full rather than half empty, we will live life more happily and tend to make a positive successful life for ourselves.

It is an aspect of character which often develops as a result of the environment in which we grow up and the people who most influence our lives. There is a joke which goes: A pessimist and optimist fell out of a tall building. As they fell past the tenth floor, the pessimist cried out, "We're going to die!" while the optimist called back, "Cheer up, we've not hit anything yet!" Clearly, although disaster is imminent, the pessimist worries all the time and expects the worst, while the optimist waits for the disaster to occur before worrying.

Whether disaster occurs or not, constant worry and anxiety are inclined to produce a pessimistic attitude to life — one which expects bad things to happen. Not only do expectations of the worst make us unhappy, if we add guilt to the picture which attributes blame to ourselves or others, that makes for a very dissatisfied life. The Indian ragpickers live in acceptance without blame and have few expectations beyond keeping their families with food. While this may not seem fulfilling, our judgement of what makes a satisfying life can result in disgust for their way of life when, really, we can admire them for their tenacity and optimism in the face of a brutal reality that life may be snuffed out at any minute.

American Psychologist and founder of the Positive Psychology Movement, Martin Seligman, has dedicated most of his life's work to understanding what brings people happiness. His book, Learned Optimism, shows us how to break the habit of imagining the worst consequences of situations, how to respond less negatively to setbacks and disappointments and how to lessen feelings of guilt. His research reveals that an optimistic attitude improves our quality of life and more encouragingly, he explains how using techniques to change our thoughts, particularly our self-talk, when difficulties arise, can boost our mood and our immune system. In short, we can learn to be optimistic with conscious awareness of our thoughts and inner dialogue.

When our glass is often half-empty with low optimism and we wish to switch to a glass half-full attitude of optimism, there are strategies to help

SWITCH STRATEGIES FOR OPTIMISM: O.P.T.I.M.I.S.M

O **Opportunities** for learning from setbacks and disappointments are optimistic outcomes of such misfortune. No one can live a life free of difficulties and unhappy events, but if we weather the storms of such troublesome times, we become stronger and more compassionate human beings. To pessimistically dwell on what is wrong in our life is to waste the time we have for fully living our best life. Switching our mindset to understanding rather than reacting to our life events is a matter of changing our thoughts from 'This is so terrible, I can't move past this!' to 'This has been terrible, but I'm so lucky to have friends to support me, and I know I can get through this even if it takes a while.'

P **Positive** expectations are excellent but sometimes we do not understand that they can be so high that we are constantly disappointed with life. When I was in my twenties, I had a friend advise me that because I expected things in my life to be 100% all the time, anything less, including 95%, would be a disappointment. He suggested that if I kept my expectations open to possibility rather than probability, even expecting 5%, I would always be happy with what little success came to me in life. This was quite a revelation to me as I realised that holding impossibly high expectations of myself and life was creating a mentality that was not helping me to be happy. Assess the level of your own expectations and explore how they are affecting your life.

T **Take action** if pessimism clouds your life. Limit time spent with negative people, and if you become aware of your energy sinking in negative thoughts, get up and move into a more positive space. I know a high-powered businessman who worked in high rise offices in a large city who used to tune in to his feelings through the workday and when he felt negativity or disappointment coming around him, he would leave the building and take a walk or find a quiet, often green, space and take himself physically to positive energy and feel more energised.

I **Inspire** yourself to focus on successes and achievements and beautiful things in life and even write them on a whiteboard in your personal space to keep them in mind. Or, if it feels right for you, buy or create posters with positive messages.

M **Move** your body and get the positive endorphins activated to keep the energy of positivity growing within. When demotivated, walk briskly; and when disheartened or dispirited, take responsibility for moving the negative feelings aside. Use visualisation techniques like imagining a warm breeze blowing through you, taking the negative energy away and switching it for exciting, positive feelings.

I **Internal dialogue** is vital for optimism. Keeping track of our thoughts and conscious awareness of our self-talk can help us identify when we are feeling negative and inform us of the need to raise our spirits into more positive territory.

S **Smile** and seek opportunities for laughter. Switch off complaints and whining and make an effort to be bright and cheerful. The old saying of 'fake it till you make it' can apply here when in situations where there is a need to be optimistic even in the face of disappointment. It is important to realise that this does not mean we put on a happy face all the time, no matter what, or that we do not genuinely express our sadder feelings. We have friends and family with whom we share our deepest fears, sadness and disappointments, and this is necessary for a balanced life; but these feelings are not for everybody around us whenever they appear. We have a family friend who wears her pessimism and negativity as if it was her permanent coat. She always comes to gatherings and events, prefers to sit alone looking glum and hardly speaking while expecting others to approach her. It has been like this for so long that no one talks to her now because her energy is like poison. Who wants this at a family occasion?

M   **Mantras** can be helpful to convince us to switch our thoughts because of their idealistic nature. Mantras are words or phrases that bring focus and concentration to an idea or feeling we wish to encourage. A simple mantra might be: 'I am too positive to be doubtful, too optimistic to be fearful and too determined to be defeated.' (@IamaJamaican). Another is: 'The days that break me are the days that make me.' Yet another very often quoted one: 'This too shall pass.' Mantras can be spoken aloud regularly, written down in sight, or used as a journaling starter. We can also make up our own mantras.

20

P. Passion Quotient

HOW GOOD ARE YOU AT MAKING TIME TO DO WHAT YOU LOVE?

Still passionate at any age

Andrew could never get enough sport in his life. As a little boy, he played football, cricket, basketball and swam each week.

Now, at 73 years of age, he still works full time and rises at 4:30 am to get to the gym by 5 am. He works out with weights and cardio exercises every day and puts top priority on his health by exercising and eating healthily. He is beyond playing competitive sport but still passionately follows sport teams and attends sporting events.

This is a passion that has never left him all his life. As a child, he would joke with his siblings, exclaiming, 'My body will keep going when your brains stop working!' I can imagine Andrew in the future, charging down the corridors of an aged home in his later years possibly beating all the staff running along behind him! His passion is inspiring.

PASSION QUOTIENT

The extent to which opportunity is made for doing something we love

Why are passions important? To pursue an activity that we love brings joy and exuberant energy into our lives and fills us with a sense of purpose. There is nothing more enriching for the heart and soul than spending time on something we feel passionate about. It makes life worthwhile, and it takes us to that feeling of awe and wonder.

We are happier doing something we enjoy and, most often, we love what we are good at as well, so we feel a sense of achievement and success when we give time and energy to our passions.

Our love for the activity also brings us into the incredibly motivating state of 'flow' that is a feeling of total absorption in something such that hours fly by without us thinking about time. Whether it is sport and exercise, as with Andrew above, or our passion is music, art, construction, reading, collecting things or outdoor pursuits, it matters not; the importance of having an interest which stirs us deeply is that we feel the energy of inspiration just by engaging with our passion.

We all remember the best teachers because of the passion they had for their subject. Their ability to arouse our enthusiasm was often the catalyst for our own learning and, in some cases, they inspired us to find our own passions in life. One such music teacher inspired me to devote much of my life's energy to singing and listening to music. Other teachers have helped young people discover their dreams through the study of subjects first encountered at school.

Without a passionate interest, life can become monotonous and less exciting. People with passion are interesting and full of energy, and some passionate people can even be a bit crazy and delightful. It is worth finding what your passions are and making time to explore them, for you never know where they might lead — even to the best job of your life.

There are some helpful strategies to switch on a passionate interest if we are lacking an interest that inspires us

SWITCH STRATEGIES TO FIND YOUR PASSION: A.W.E.

A **Answer** your heart's calling. Tune in to all the things that bring joy and excitement into your life and make time for them as often as possible. A little time every day for a pleasurable activity can change your life from ordinary happiness to extraordinary delight.

W **Wonder** what you might discover as a passion if you simply googled things or activities of interest. If you have had an inkling to find out more about something, make time for it, connect with other people who know about it and give it a go. It may or may not lead to something great! Risk being good (or not!) at something.

E **Education** courses are a brilliant source of discovering interesting passions. Not only are there the most abundant collection of online courses, but webinars and podcasts are also so popular because they can be turned on immediately or they can fill a spare hour or two whenever you are free. As well as online activities, there are many short courses of hours or a few weeks that you can attend to meet like-minded people and study with an expert for a small fee. I have done many such courses in pursuit of interests and discovered new talents and passions such as floristry, painting, interior design, and aromatherapy. Each of these has given me hours of pleasure and a few new skills to enrich my life. Go and find your passions!

21

Q. Questionability Quotient

HOW WELL DO YOU USE QUESTIONS IN YOUR LIFE?

What lies beneath the surface?

Sixteen-year-old Tim was lurking at my office door, clearly waiting to be spotted rather than taking the initiative to knock. Luckily, I did catch sight of him and opened the door with a warm 'Hi' and a friendly, welcoming smile. I then invited him in to sit down.

When I asked what had brought him there, he told me he needed some help with 'study skills'. Of course, here was a simple situation because I had plenty of resources to help him get organised for study and exams. But I did not launch into the solution. Instead, I gently asked him what was stopping him from studying. He replied that he was 'finding it hard to concentrate'.

I continued to follow his clues by asking why he was not able to think about his work. He hesitated before stating that he had some problems that were taking his mind off study. I then observed and commented that he seemed pretty stressed. I told him that it can be difficult to study when other things are more worrying. At this moment, tears sprang into his eyes, and I could tell how distressed he was feeling.

'Why are you hurting so much Tim?' I asked with concern. On this question, he began to tell the story of the break-up of his first love relationship. This was disappointing enough, but he was particularly devastated for not only had the girl broken up with him, but she had gone off with another boy and then spread negative and confidential information about Tim's personal life to other students. He felt betrayed and worthless.

The tears freely flowed for a long time as he recounted the details of his personal disaster. He needed to express and understand the grief situation more deeply. It was in later counselling sessions that we were able to focus on the problem preventing Tim from studying. This situation indicates how powerful the right questions can be in helping us get the information we may need to understand issues more fully. If we also ask ourselves the right questions, we can uncover our intense feelings and gain personal insights into our own lives.

QUESTIONABILITY QUOTIENT

The ability to think of and ask insightful questions of self and others

Good questions are vital for excellent communication. Combine a helpful question with positive listening behaviour and you will have the tools for good communication in relationships for life. They do not simply provide information, although this seems to be the primary purpose of questions, but they also open interesting new topics and lead discussions to exciting directions we may not have anticipated. Through extending conversations, questions help us build positive relationships based on deeper understanding.

The most powerful questions we can ask are the **open-ended questions** that begin with words such as:

Who? What? When? Where? Why? How?

I call these the 'W + H' questions, and they are what we call open-ended questions because they welcome extra information compared with closed questions beginning with words like Is, Are, Can, and Do, which tend to receive 'Yes' or 'No' answers. If we ask someone, 'Are you going out?' The most likely answer from this closed question is 'Yes' or 'No' and the conversation may stop there. If we ask, 'Where are you going?' it encourages the person to elaborate a little more in their answer. There is a greater incentive to expand the answer which can lead to another question or a mutual sharing of plans.

One of the best-selling books of all time, and perhaps the

first of the true self-help books, was written by Dale Carnegie and published in 1936. Its enticing title is *How to Win Friends and Influence People*. Reading this book as a teenager at school changed my life and began a lifelong passion for learning about personal development. His basic advice is that by asking people questions about themselves, taking a genuine interest in them and really listening carefully, we engender friendship with them. It makes them like us and creates a connection which can be a pathway to friendship. I learned the power of taking an interest in people and found that it became the way to develop positive relationships of mutual sharing. It takes practice and thought to frame the best questions to discover the ideas of other people, but it is one of life's most valuable skills.

To develop a good questionability quotient,
we can learn some strategies which can improve
our relationships

SWITCH STRATEGIES FOR QUESTIONABILITY: A.S.K.

A **Ask** open-ended questions when talking with others, whether with friends or in work meetings. They encourage people to talk and share much more fully. Consciously think about the questions you ask so that you help others to explain or elaborate on their answers or ideas.

S **Spend time** asking questions about the person with whom you are passing time. Listen carefully to the answers, and then respond appropriately. Dale

Carnegie (author above) believed that people love to talk about themselves to someone who will listen. The most effective way to make friends is to show interest in someone you meet. If all you do is talk about yourself, others may consider you self-centred and very uninteresting. Think about the people you have met in your life who always talk about themselves and never ask you about your life or your opinions. The best conversations are two-sided with each person interested in each other's ideas and life stories.

K **Know** how to listen well. Look at the person, nod or smile in response to statements appropriately and make empathetic comments such as: 'That must have been fabulous!' or 'That sounds terrible!' This shows people that we are really listening sincerely and that we understand their feelings. This response is also worth practising as often as possible.

22

R. Resilience Quotient

HOW WELL DO YOU RECOVER FROM DIFFICULTY?

From Darkness into Light

Jane had many reasons to be sorry for herself, but she was not! She could occasionally allow herself to fall into a quagmire and have a deep soulful cry, but she never stayed there and never allowed herself to sink into such sorrow from which she could not come back. She was warm and generous-hearted, helpful to everyone and one of the most resilient, positive people I have ever met.

She had feared she might die at the hands of a violent first husband from whom she escaped with her life and went into hiding. A few years later, with a new, loving husband, her life looked as if it was on track positively until they experienced the loss of six babies — just before or a few weeks after birth. This left them childless and accepting of their situation, until unexpectedly, Jane found herself having a baby at 40. The joy of a miracle baby who actually lived was a huge blessing, and life was good until her husband died early and quickly of kidney cancer. So much seemed to be challenging her very sanity as she experienced ups followed by downs of severe magnitude. There was loneliness and stress from these life tragedies and difficulties. She experienced many times of darkness.

But Jane was such an amazingly resilient and positive person that she allowed her grief to express itself for a time before re-energising herself and moving on with life.

She moved to a new suburb, rejuvenated her teaching career, took up studies in languages, and even bought a sailing boat to teach herself how to sail! Jane began to seek and find new interests and social connections.

She went out to make a fulfilling life, despite the tragedies that had befallen her, and she had an energy of joyfulness, humour and laughter that pervaded her whole personality, drawing people to her in a magnetic way. She talked to people in the street, shopkeepers and little children in the park, sharing little friendly moments everywhere. Everyone loved Jane because she was good company, and she would rush to the aid of needy people with whom she came in contact.

Whenever she felt lonely or down, she would quote the old saying: 'Count your blessings every day and name them one by one.' She remains, to this day, the most resilient person I have ever known because of her capacity to grieve for the losses but not get stuck in distress. By reflecting consciously with gratitude for what is good in her life, she has been able, time and time again, to re-charge her energy and change her life direction to create a positive life, no matter what crisis appeared at the door.

RESILIENCE QUOTIENT

The ability to get up and get going after disappointment or failure

Our capacity to recover within a reasonable time from difficulties, disappointments and adversities, as well as catastrophes such as the grief of loss or serious illness, is a huge benefit of living a positive life.

We all know that life is a complex pattern of ups and downs, of joy and sadness, of successes and failure; with regret and celebration woven into daily existence. While we all keep hoping terrible things will never happen to us, most of us understand that troubles may be just around the corner for us all. When people have life-threatening experiences or times that challenge all their existential beliefs, it is common to reassess life as it is and begin to look for a transformed life.

This is seen most commonly when the life challenge becomes so great that it leads us to what has been known for centuries as a 'Dark Night of the Soul' — a time of utter desolation, disconnection and emptiness in which a person can feel hopeless and deeply depressed. Eckhart Tolle has written about this phenomenon and suggests that it is a state of being in which life seems meaningless. It can be triggered by an event or circumstance in which 'the meaning you had given your life, your activities, your achievements, where you are going, what is considered important... for some reason, collapses'. He further explains that after this experience, 'there is a possibility that you emerge out of that into a transformed state of consciousness' in which 'life has meaning again but it's no longer a conceptual meaning that you can necessarily explain' and you 'awaken into something which is deeper' with a 'deeper sense of purpose'.

Becoming resilient does not mean that we shrug off our grief, pain and sorrow, 'put on a happy face', and quickly move forward with life. In contrast, it means that we experience all the extreme emotions fully before resetting our lives on a future pathway. Robert Holden's wonderfully wise and very readable book, *Shift Happens*, explains that we should feel our 'feelings all the way through to the other side' because a 'feeling…(just) wants to be felt'. In his work on 'The Happiness Project', he believes we need 'to be honest' about how we feel, and he advises us to 'keep smiling — unless you feel like crying'. But herein lies the difficulty, for feeling is the healing process, but to feel resilient enough to keep living positively, we have to let go of feelings because the result of clinging and holding on to feelings is pain and suffering. For resilience, we have to be prepared to lose our suffering and re-engage with life.

Getting over everyday disappointments is not as challenging as 'The Dark Night of the Soul' scenarios, but for some people, it still presents a challenge. Some positive steps can be taken to help us on our way through dark clouds in order to find some silver linings.

When our Resilience Quotient needs enhancing, there are helpful behaviours to get us back into a positive life space.

SWITCH STRATEGIES FOR RESILIENCE: G.E.T.U.P. & G.O.

G **Grow Self-Awareness** so you can recognise when your mood or confidence is slipping and take early steps to Nurture yourself in your own way and to Problem Solve for the situation that is unfolding. A helpful exercise in problem solving is the old but good Brainstorm of ideas (alone or with a trusted friend) on large sheets of paper. This opens the mind to options and is a positive step towards action.

E **Embrace Change** and see the opportunities that new settings, actions, people and activities can bring. Find new interests that encourage a Sense of Purpose by helping others who are less fortunate or by discovering new pursuits and passions.

T **Turn Up Each Day** as far as possible and find ways to get going rather than allow yourself to run away and hide for long periods of time. I have memories of working in some terrible negative work environments with people who had no compunction about hurting and rejecting others, and I had to get up each morning to face this atmosphere. It was depressing and debilitating. Over many years working in schools, I met some particularly destructive and cynical teachers who had no business working with kids, and it was even harder for those young people to turn up and face such teachers day after day. In these kinds of circumstances, I had two plans: firstly, to talk to myself about my own confidence each morning, put on a brave face and turn up no matter what happened; and secondly, to seek new possible work to get me out of these situations.

U   **Ups & Downs** are part of life, and we almost have to imagine life as a roller coaster that we can't completely control. Sometimes we just have to hold on and keep our eyes looking to the front. The more we ride the Life-coaster, the more practiced we become at holding on tightly. This is resilience, and it helps us be more flexible, increasing our stability in the changing landscape of Life.

P   **Positive Self-talk and Action** are both needed when we feel challenged by circumstances. A student whom I saw in counselling who was going through huge self-doubt found it helpful to write notes to himself and stick them all over his bedroom wall as reminders of his skills and abilities. He wrote down sayings and encouraging song lyrics to remind himself to believe in his strengths. Having special songs or words can help us raise our energy and support our emotional well-being.

&

G   **Goals** can become very helpful for raising our energy and getting us into action. Both short-term and long-term goals can clarify our hopes and dreams and generate enough enthusiasm to stir us out of a 'stuck' position into an action mode.

- **Out and About** is the way to connect with the world! If we are lonely or hoping to find new friends or a life partner, for example, we cannot wait in expectation that there will be a knock at the door and the right person will be there. We have to make a choice to reach out and develop a strong social network. In doing so, we become more resilient as we try and try again to connect with others.

23

S. Sociability Quotient

HOW WELL DO YOU MANAGE RELATIONSHIPS?

Everybody's a friend

Sam' social instincts were incredible! I once saw him send out a social media message to 100 people on Saturday, inviting them to meet for a BBQ because it was going to be a sunny Sunday. Sixty people turned up at 24 hours' notice!

That is a person who has a high sociability quotient!

But what made Sam so popular?

It was his natural ability to get to know people by approaching them at social functions and making positive connections with them. He did not wait for others to come to him; rather, he found his way to people and showed genuine interest in them. He also connected them to other people in his ever-widening circle of friends. Sam had travelled all over the world, both with friends and alone, for months at a time; he had been a tour guide in Europe when he was just 24, escorting busloads of 50 young people at a time for Contiki Tours; then he had been successful as a top sales executive. All of these jobs relied on his exceptional personal relationship skills.

All the while, his social life blossomed as the years went by. Not only was he sociable, but he had a great sense of humour, an accepting attitude and an optimistic outlook on life.

SOCIABILITY QUOTIENT

The ability to make and keep social connections with people

The ability to relate to people and form positive relationships, as in the case of Sam above, cannot be underestimated as a valuable characteristic. While this is often a natural personality trait, there are ways of developing our sociability quotient. Skills in communication are central to being able to negotiate our relationships successfully. If we can consciously reflect on our relationships — whether with friends, family or lovers — we have multiple opportunities to improve and develop our sociability during our lifetime. What are the sociability skills we need to be great at relationship building?

Listening and speaking skills are the most vital elements of any relationship. The Vietnamese monk, Thich Nhat Hanh (pronounced Tick-Naught-Han), in his *The Miracle of Mindfulness*, revealed that if you are in a conversation or a meeting, be fully aware that this is what you are doing and give your attention to the person in front of you. Don't be thinking about something else. We have all experienced what it feels like to talk with someone who seems to be flashing their eyes elsewhere or hardly responding with any facial reactions when we speak to them. Another annoying behaviour comes from the person who wants to interrupt: the frustrating one who seems only to be waiting for the chance to cut into your story to tell their own which seems much more important than yours. This is the quickest way to turn others off and send them looking for someone else in the room with whom to spend time. Only through open-hearted listening and genuine interest in others can we be caring humans who respond sensitively to other people.

There is a beautiful Celtic expression called 'Anam Cara' which means "soul friend" and which refers to the kind of friend with whom we can share our innermost self. While we do not wish to have this kind of friendship with everyone, we are missing out if we cannot count at least one anam cara in our lifetime. A most beautiful book of the same title by John O'Donohue explores the concept of Anam Cara and shows us the value of letting our negative personality traits reveal aspects of ourselves through greater self-awareness. While we do not want to over analyse our inner selves, by listening to the 'refined antennae' of the soul, we can deepen our enrichment of life and experience its mystery. With greater awareness of our need to listen to others, we can connect more consciously and deepen our relationships.

Questioning skills are invaluable when meeting new people, both socially and professionally. Asking people how they are going and expanding their answers with further questions encourages people to speak about themselves (which most people enjoy doing) and shows them that we are genuinely interested in their lives.

A flexible and affable attitude to life allows people to feel confident that we can respond to them with friendliness and respect. There are some people we meet who are 'tricky' to deal with because we never know whether they will be positive and polite or annoyed and rejecting of our suggestions. These people easily 'burn' their relationships because they behave unpredictably and sometimes even abusively. People tend to avoid them in the workplace because they upset their colleagues and, in their personal lives, they tend not to have many friends because they will not compromise on what they want to do, nor will they listen to and accept other's opinions. If we always put our interests and opinions first, we can be sure that people will dislike us enough to avoid us. If we also react angrily or speak sharply to others, they will usually react by moving out of our orbit. We see this often with difficult, disrespectful relationships in which partners 'snipe' and 'snap' at one another, putting down the opinions and ideas of the other person. This is a form of emotional abuse which erodes relationships over many years.

Being kind and supportive to our fellow humans is a conscious behaviour approach that reaps great rewards in terms of friendship and loving relationships. How little it takes to be kind and supportive rather than dismissive and destructive to others. How much difference it makes to reach out with a listening ear and a warm heart to those who have been negatively targeted by others and those who are lonely. Our sociability quotient is not only about our skills in positively relating to people in our immediate orbit but also about our generosity and kindness to the less fortunate. I know a man who frequently engages in genuine conversations with homeless individuals as he walks through the city, not only giving them money but asking them about their lives. They are so often very appreciative of someone taking an interest in their story.

In love relationships and partnerships, loving another is not just about feeling loving towards the other; it is about truly understanding how the other person feels. The only way to do this is to regularly engage in deep and meaningful conversations about life and feelings. Often, women are better at these kinds of conversations, and many women search for the kind of partner who can truly share life on a deeper level than simply talking about daily activities. Of course, meaningful conversations can't happen all the time because having fun and doing interesting things is also important, but when couples can lie in bed and pillow-talk often, they have a greater chance of keeping in touch at a deeper level.

When we feel our sociability skills could benefit from improvement, there are strategies that can help

SWITCH STRATEGIES FOR SOCIABILITY: C.O.N.T.A.C.T

C **Contact with people enriches our lives.** Don't wait for others to come to you! Go forward to greet them whenever you are in professional and social situations. If you are shy, be courageous and move towards someone who looks a little friendly and start a conversation. A little formula that can help is C.I.Q. (Compliment – Introduce yourself – Question) For example, C – 'Love the food here!' I – 'Hi, I'm -----.' Q – 'How did you come to be here?' Whatever you can think up that sounds like a plausible comment or question is worth a try. Practice many different phrases, comments and questions in different social situations. Remember, some things do not come naturally, but they can become easier with practice.

O **Observe people closely and notice their body language.** Often, we can tell how a person is feeling by the way they stand or walk or behave in different situations. People who are shy will stand back from others and may listen but not speak much. The extroverts in a room will move confidently and speak often so these people may be easier to approach. If you wish to talk with someone who is quiet, it is better not to ask questions but to make an observation such as, 'It looks like you know what you are doing!' or 'I heard you say…(repeat their comment) and I really agree with that!'

N **New relationships are worth developing.** There are many interest and hobby clubs that offer opportunities for new friendships and even love relationships. Pet-related organisations are particularly good for new social connections. Anyone who has ever walked a puppy or dog in a public place will attest to the incredible attraction that animals create as they connect with others. People naturally feel relaxed about interacting with a friendly animal and great conversations can develop. If good conversation in any social setting occurs, it is worth suggesting further interactions and following up if contacts are given. We never know where these connections lead.

T **Trust and Honesty are to be highly valued in relationships.** We all need to believe in the goodness of others and trust them to be honest and fair with us. It is important not to use people or lie about ourselves if we wish to form positive relationships. Internet dating is notoriously challenging in this way since there are quite a few unscrupulous people who hurt others with little regard for their feelings. It is also good to be brave enough to confront people with hurtful behaviours by talking things over. This may lead to deep and meaningful conversations which are very helpful for intensifying relationships as a result of heart-centred and honest sharing.

A **Attitudes of Forgiveness and Acceptance are important in close relationships.** By accepting that we all have our faults and issues, we can become more tolerant and accepting of the behaviours of others that we find challenging. Not liking the behaviour of someone does not mean we dislike the person completely. However, we do sometimes need to close down or leave relationships that are personally destructive, even when the person is a family member. It's a hard, sometimes impossible, choice to end a close relationship, but then, as the saying goes, some people come into our lives for 'a reason, a season, or a lifetime'.

C **Care and Kindness in relationships are essential for good sociability.** We all know instinctively which behaviours are kind and caring, and we also understand mean and hurtful behaviour. It is always worth remembering how we ourselves feel if others treat us unkindly. A simple phone call or message is always valued.

T **Thankfulness for the assistance our friends give us is important.** We all need appreciation for any help we give others so we should remember the small gestures of friendship — a thank-you message, a small gift or a nice card is always valued greatly.

24

T. Thankfulness Quotient

HOW OFTEN DO YOU 'COUNT YOUR BLESSINGS'?

Simple Gratitude

I remember a family counselling session with parents and their two sons in which the elder son churlishly complained and whined that he did not have the best of the 'branded' skateboards. He didn't like his cheaper alternative! His father answered him by declaring he would 'give away the skateboard' and his son could 'do without'!

By contrast, in the seldom-visited remote villages of India lie some of the poorest people on earth; but some of the most grateful people imaginable. There is a tiny school, one of many, high up in the Himalayas, which operates on donations from generous locals. Many of the families survive on only what they grow for food and what they can earn from making reed baskets to sell at the town market. Husbands have often deserted their families or died and left mothers and children to fend alone.

In this little school, I have a memory of giving a gift of coloured pencils and drawing books to each child and feeling overwhelmed at the sight of the small faces lighting up with beaming smiles to receive this simplest of gestures. Thankfulness was here in joyful faces with smiling eyes. Gratitude was revealed in excitement for small things of little monetary value.

For me, there was pleasure flowing back to me for making others happy with my giving. There was thankfulness for the opportunity this experience gave me to see how fortunate my life has been in comparison. Above all, there was the encouragement to focus on the positive elements of life rather than becoming stuck with the tangling weeds of life's adverse situations.

In many areas of the world, particularly in Asian and African nations where great numbers of the population are poor, there is evidence of great appreciation for small things, and while there is no doubt that there is great need, it is also amazing to experience great gratitude. We, in the affluent West, could certainly learn much about the power of thankfulness.

THE THANKFULNESS QUOTIENT

The capacity for 'living' gratitude in our daily lives

We all understand what thankfulness and gratitude is, but many people hardly practice it in their daily lives. The mystic and poet Rumi implores us to 'hear blessings dropping their blossoms around us', and an old Estonian Proverb reminds us that the person 'who does not thank for little will not thank for much'. How common it is to see people living with a narrow definition of gratitude which simply involves saying thank you when given a gift or when someone performs an act of kindness for us. There is so much more to living with an 'Attitude of Gratitude' in daily life.

Thankfulness involves *FIVE ASPECTS OF GRATITUDE*

1. A generous spoken, written or demonstrated 'Thank you' for gifts and acts of kindness.

2. An outlook on life that appreciates the learning which comes from facing adversity.

3. A capacity to notice and genuinely appreciate small, seemingly insignificant things, such as a wildflower or babbling creek.

4. A way of living mindfully and gratefully that highlights what is good, beautiful and positive rather than focusing on what is wrong with life and the world.

5. A daily conscious practice of gratitude which begins and ends each day to reinforce a positive mood and increase happiness.

Implementing these Five Aspects has been shown to decrease depression and increase our happiness. The Positive Psychology movement initiated by Martin Seligman and researched by his team of associates has provided clear and unequivocal evidence of the power of gratitude to change our mindset in such a way that our emotions are enhanced positively.

His school of Positive Psychology created a new dynamic approach to helping people by seeking not to focus on what is wrong with them but to discover and enhance what is right with them. His investigations help people look for their 'Strengths' rather than their weaknesses and in so doing, they learn to be grateful for what is going well in their lives, thus creating increased happiness. He helps people not only to seek happiness through a 'pleasurable life' (e.g. doing things we love, like watching movies or eating out) but also by participating in an 'engaged life' of activities that inspire and elevate our strengths, as well as contributing to a 'meaningful life' in which we help others. All of these have elements of gratitude for what life brings us in daily life and in the longer term.

Some cultures show us how to make an attitude of gratitude part of our everyday life. In wandering the laneways in Bali, I marvelled at the beautiful but simple altars that every shop and household created anew each day. It was common to see a bowl of water with items such as flowers, a lighted candle and a feather representing the elements of water, earth, fire and air — sitting at the entrance to a home or business. This small gesture provided a reminder that every day, there is a need to feel gratitude, even for the smallest blessings. Not only was there thankfulness for what had already been received but also gratitude for the blessings imagined in the coming day. It may have also been connected with the spiritual gods, of course, but nevertheless, these visible gestures of appreciation remind us not only to be thankful for getting what we want but also to be grateful for whatever might come our way in the future.

When we wish for our Thankfulness Quotient to increase our happiness, there are strategies that can be helpful

SWITCH STRATEGIES FOR THANKFULNESS: T.H.A.N.K.S

T **Thank-you expressions are important.** Whether it is within our family, our friends or work colleagues, personal expressions of gratitude are so enriching for those in receipt of the sentiment. We should not forget to make this a priority in life. For me, carefully chosen cards and thoughtful words are much more important than gifts as expressions of love and connection.

H **Handling adversity by being grateful for life-learning is beneficial.** Being able to get past the difficulties and being grateful for small wins or personal insights is healthy for a positive life. It's the old saying 'Count your blessings; name them one by one' concept that allows us to see beyond complete self-destruction. Nevertheless, in the case of total despair, as likely with the violent death of a loved one, this concept is hard to imagine as having any positive outcome. People who believe in the afterlife seem to take comfort in the possibility of meeting up with loved ones after death.

A **Appreciating small things and even recording them in a gratitude diary is uplifting.** Daily observations of beautiful, inspiring items or events can lift us into happier, more relaxed states of feeling. Seeking the sunrise or sunset and simply enjoying the breathtaking spectacle is a cause for celebrating each day that we have to be alive. Make a list of what you find awe-inspiring and try to catch one of these every day!

N **Noticing the positive rather than focusing on the negative experiences of life is more enriching.** Seeing disappointments and challenges as an inevitable part of life not only helps us feel better but also lifts the energy of those around us.

K **Keeping gratitude in mind daily raises our positive energy.** It has been shown by Martin Seligman's vast research studies that if we remain mindful of thanks throughout the day, we can change the brainwaves and our emotional energy. To wake up and express thanks openly by speaking gratitude aloud (For example, 'I am grateful for a warm bed, a good night's sleep, and a delicious breakfast.') starts our day positively. Last thing at night, before bed, the same idea works to look for the things of the day for which we can be grateful, and this helps our brain and body relax for sleep.

S **Seeing the world as bountiful and beautiful and looking for the good in people is to be treasured and**

cultivated. Khalil Gibran's timeless philosophy of life in The Prophet reminds us to pray not only in times of distress but also in times of 'joy' and 'abundance'. He suggests that gratitude for the gift of life can be forgotten when everything is going well, and we may pray for help in dark times but forget to be thankful for good times. The Balinese practice of creating an abundant focus is about always expecting the best, in good times and in bad. Try setting up a small centre of beauty in your own home or work environment: a simple flower from the garden; a smooth pebble; a beautiful bowl or sculpture in a prominent place; or a gift from a loved one can remind us daily to feel grateful.

25

U. Understanding Quotient

HOW WELL DO YOU UNDERSTAND YOURSELF AND OTHERS?

How can we go deeper?

It was about a year after they were first together that Jacklyn realised a problem with her relationship. They enjoyed doing things together and had fun, but something was missing. She didn't realise what was wrong for her until they moved in together and she tried to talk to him about important issues on a deep level.

Tim was a great companion — intelligent, interesting and caring, with great values — and many girls might be very satisfied with this, but not Jacklyn. She wanted more depth in their sharing, and she wanted them to understand each other better — to grow as individuals. He seemed happy to remain connected on a superficial level and he wished for her to be happy simply sitting and watching TV with him or cooking meals as required. She longed to read and discuss books with him, share thoughts about the world, and particularly, talk about the challenges of her work. He didn't discuss his work or ask her about her job; nor did he read much or take an interest in current affairs.

They both had difficulty understanding and accepting the person with whom they now found themselves intimately connected. For her part, Jacklyn realised that she had chosen someone whom she found to be shallow and who related to the world in a different way from her while Tim felt confused because he simply loved her and didn't know what he needed to be or do for Jacklyn.

The gap in the understanding between Jacklyn and Tim was becoming a chasm.

UNDERSTANDING QUOTIENT

The ability to understand people and situations

We may wonder why we need such a characteristic as 'understanding' to improve our life, but in many ways, this is the vital glue that keeps relationships positive. 'Understanding' is not the simplistic 'knowing what a person wants, needs or feels' but rather the 'deep acceptance of the inner world of another', whatever that may be. When couples, family members and friends believe someone does not understand them, the gulf between them grows larger until the desire to explore each person's inner world becomes shattered. This is what leads to break-ups and human dislocation.

When we truly seek to understand another person, we

often face the challenge of wading through their past experiences, present situations and future expectations. We are sometimes faced with shocks and distress at hearing the true inner feelings of another. At any moment, we are all influenced by what life is presenting to us, and it is often fiendishly difficult to get to the heart of another person. But having deeper, meaningful conversations about our very essence as humans and sharing our gravest fears as well as our loftiest dreams enriches our self-understanding while bringing us closer together with those we love. This is what Jacklyn (above) desired in her relationship with Tim, but she suspected he was not inclined or not able to fulfil that need within her.

As Counsellors, engaged to sift through the human issues we all face, we strive each day to meet that challenge of understanding other human beings. This is why the counsellor who does not have a perfect life but one who has experienced many of life's tribulations can often more easily access and accept the very worst that a person can express. Successful understanding relies on both the listener really hearing the individual who is speaking their heart and that individual being prepared to reveal at the deepest level some possible wounds from the past without denying the issues at hand.

Being open to a deeper understanding of ourselves and others is the doorway to improving relationships. As soon as we become defensive about ourselves justifying why something happened, we lose our capacity for the self-reflection and growth necessary to create the possibility for change. And if someone who is deeply connected to us begins to understand how we feel and refuses to try and change, it is time to make a choice to continue the relationship or end the chapter with that character in our lives.

There is a plethora of books and articles that help people with understanding in relationships. Everything that gives us even one insight or idea for new ways of seeing others better is worth receiving. Allan and Barbara Pease have written extensively on understanding body language which is very helpful when meeting new people.

For established relationships, the book *The Five Love Languages* by Gary Chapman is enlightening as an insight into understanding how individuals express love differently. He outlines five ways in which people see themselves demonstrating their love for another. They are: 1. Words of Affirmation; 2. Acts of Service; 3. Receiving Gifts; 4. Quality Time; 5. Physical Touch. Chapman reveals that by understanding another person's way of expressing love in one of these ways, we can share similarities and differences and become more accepting of the other, as well as learn how to return love in ways most understood by the other person. For example, if one person performs acts of service (cleaning the house, mowing the lawns, etc.) or gives gifts as a sign of love, but the other person needs words of affirmation ('You look fantastic!') and physical touch (Hugs), they may fail to understand each other's 'languages' of love.

Sharing what each person needs can help them understand better how to support the relationship.

We may think the act of understanding other people and

situations seems like a rudimentary skill, but it is not. Author Dale Carnegie reminds us that 'Any fool can criticise, condemn, and complain but it takes character and self-control to be understanding and forgiving.' Former US President Lyndon Johnson once reminded us that 'If we are to live together in peace, we must come to know each other better.' There is no underestimating the power of deeper understanding as a window into the soul of another and as a bridge to a stronger connection with everyone we encounter.

When we feel we lack understanding to a high degree, we can engage with strategies that may assist us to deepen our insights into others

SWITCH STRATEGIES: LISTEN. ACCEPT. UNDERSTAND. SHARE

LISTEN with patience, allowing the other person to be heard without interruption. There is nothing worse than someone cutting us off when we are mid-sentence or have not finished speaking. Active listening means we are looking at the person and we are also giving them our heart's attention. We can show interest and seek clarification by asking occasional questions and nodding, where appropriate. Our aim is to truly understand what is being expressed from the other person's heart to ours. It is especially helpful to ask the person how they are 'feeling'.

The language of Listening is: *'I hear what you are saying.'* And *'Tell me more about that/ why you think that/how you feel...'* Sometimes, we can repeat what we have heard, *'You seem to feel...'*

ACCEPT what is being shared in the first instance, no matter what it is and whether you believe it to be true or not because there will be a time later for challenging the person's views and impressions. Resist the urge to argue back and become defensive about what the other person is saying, especially if it is personal feedback.

The language of Acceptance is: *'I'm sorry that you have been angry and upset or hurt and disappointed...'* And *'I now understand better what you have been feeling.'*

UNDERSTAND the person's message and their feelings since sometimes the feeling is more important than the message. Listening and accepting the message and the feeling is what understanding is all about. When we show that we understand, it diffuses the intensity of feelings and opens the door to more honest sharing and even to challenging of viewpoints. If we need to take issue with the other person's perceptions, it is helpful to stay calm and state our reason for disagreement very clearly. It does not mean we need to be free of emotion, but loud, angry or abusive emotional outbursts lead nowhere but to more anger and escalating verbal violence.

The language of Understanding and Challenge is: *'I understand how you may have thought that/felt that... but I did not mean what I said in that way. What I wanted to say to you was...'* And *'I am disappointed/surprised/ upset that you did/said that... because it makes me feel... also.'* By staying calm, despite strong emotions, there is an opportunity for open and honest discussion.

SHARE points of view and feelings. When we consciously consider how well we have understood the feelings, motivations, problems and life experiences of another, we have elevated our own capacity for personal growth. Similarly, when we discuss differences of opinion or understanding of events, we increase the depth of the interactions within our relationships. However, understanding does not mean convincing another person to do as we wish — for each of us has the choice and responsibility of our own beliefs and actions. By seeking to find a position of mutual understanding, or at least having the desire to understand, relationships can grow. There is the possibility of strengthening and improving all kinds of personal and professional relationships. Finally, the conversations that involve greater understanding can become those 'deep and meaningful' interactions that we may never forget.

26

V. Visualization Quotient

HOW WELL DO YOU VISUALIZE YOUR FUTURE?

Making the future

Many years ago, I learned the art of visualizing from a couple who practiced their ideas for creating the future they wanted.

Each January, Anna and James would leave their three children with grandparents for the day while they went to a local shopping centre food court to set up a corner and work together on visualizing their lives for the coming year. With coffees and treats, they would share and write feelings, ideas, goals and plans. They would begin by asking each other the question: What would you like to see, feel, achieve and do this year? It was an exercise that they enjoyed enormously, and they felt it energised them to set goals and take action steps to maximise their enjoyment of life.

I began doing this same exercise but added extra elements to the process prior to beginning, including meditation. This was a way of setting my intention for the outcome. Over the years in which I have engaged in this visualization ritual, I feel I have seen many amazing dreams and goals come to fruition. My husband and I now plan a weekend escape to the mountains or ocean each year, and with coloured felt pens and large sheets of paper, we visualize our future. We created a new life in the countryside and found the house we had imagined, as well as successfully designing a life that incorporated family, work, new interests and new friendships. We feel blessed to be able to continue to live the rich life we visualized and imagined. We believe that everyone can positively imagine a wonderful life.

VISUALIZATION QUOTIENT

The capacity to use visualization to inspire a good life

So often, I hear people say, 'I am no good at visualizing' because they say they cannot imagine or see what is invisible or what is not tangible to them. Yet, these same people read books which is all about visualizing places, characters and events. Visualization is simply the formation of a mental image of something.

Taken further, it is the visual representation of objects, situations and images arranged on paper, on a screen or a board in such a way that may include pictures, symbols, words, colours, and diagrams. It is a process that can be practiced and that can be creatively developed according to individual insights. For example, an artist might use only pictures for visualisation, or a person with word skills may use verse, while a mathematician may enjoy creating new symbols and equations to represent the imagined visions and goals.

Why is visualization a powerful practice to develop?

Firstly, it is excellent for stimulating our brains to go beyond passive acceptance of what is obvious to active creation of new images and ideas. Inventors are never short of ideas because of their ability to use visualizations to create something that can solve a problem of some kind or another.

Secondly, it helps us uncover and express some of our deeper desires, allowing us to 'play with new possibilities' even if we never activate or achieve them.

Thirdly, it increases our motivation to work towards goals or to succeed at something we wish to achieve. Athletes and performers have used visualization techniques for many years as a way of helping them better their performances and achieve greatness. A sprinter who visualizes herself/himself going past the finish line first, hearing the roar of the crowd, sensing the pride and joy of receiving a trophy and achieving success is increasing motivation and creating fresh incentives.

Finally, visualization activates the Law of Attraction, which is the ability to attract into our lives whatever we are focusing on. It uses the power of the mind to translate whatever is in our thoughts and materialize them into reality.

If we constantly think negatively and focus on bad things happening, they often do; but if we look for good things, even in bad situations, we will invariably find something to appreciate. There is a well-known story of actor Jim Carrey — before he was famous — writing himself a cheque for $10 million for services for acting and keeping it in his wallet. Ten years later, he was offered the role in Dumb and Dumber for $10 million. This is visualisation in a tangible form.

The concept of the Law of Attraction is so often viewed by sceptics and cynics as 'mumbo jumbo hippie stuff' because it IS difficult to believe. And of course, what you believe comes back to you, so those who have found this Law to be helpful are those who have believed enough, while the sceptics will never have evidence because they do not live as if the Law of Attraction works. So many scientists, especially quantum physicists, have now proven the existence of a powerful energy field connecting us all to others and the natural world around us. Whether we believe in this Law or not, visualization can still be a helpful future-life motivator.

If we wish to improve our ability to use visualisation as an inspiration for a good life, there are strategies that can be selected and applied

SWITCH STRATEGIES: DREAM. IMAGINE. VISUALIZE. BELIEVE

DREAM your life. Set aside time to create a process of your own choosing to visualise and represent your 'Fulfilled Life'. You might use a large piece of paper, a whiteboard or an electronic device to record your ideas and 'visions'. You might include photos, cut-out pictures and words from magazines, symbols, phrases, drawings, poetry, raw materials from nature — whatever ideas come to you! Include some goals and plans for your work, home environment and your relationships. Invite someone to share this experience with you as well — either to help you or to create their own life vision. Make it a joyful, interesting experience of freedom and fun.

IMAGINE you in your FULFILLED LIFE. Close your eyes and imagine you are watching a film of your future 'Fulfilled Life': visualize all the aspects you would like to see come to you. Imagine how you will feel, what you will be doing differently, which people will be around you and what they will be saying to you.

VISUALISE the future in reality. Set a time in your mind for these things to begin happening and *buy a notebook with a page for each envisioned goal to record:*

1. What I need to do to start the process of achieving each goal or dream: for example, 'In order to fall in love, I need to find new ways of meeting someone.'

2. The signs that I will be looking for to show that change is happening: for example, 'I have joined a new social club/started a new course or hobby.'

3. Words of gratitude for any small achievements, successes, or signs of change for the better: for example, 'I am grateful that I enjoyed the social group, even though I did not meet a "special someone".'

BELIEVE in the possibilities that life presents. Many, many times in my counselling experiences, I sat with people who had lost hope of being happy, and I reminded them that even though you can't see around the next corner, it doesn't mean that something amazing is not waiting for you there. Sometimes in our life, we see the road ahead as if it were a clearly viewed straight road with more of the same that we are experiencing at present, but life has many turns and corners and different roads going in many directions. There is always the possibility of a life change at any time. One day can make a huge difference in our life. Hanging on when times are tough is important but taking responsibility for visualizing a different life is a good strategy for stopping us from being victims of life. We can visualise the turns in the road and believe in the possibilities until they come into reality.

27

W. Well-being Quotient

HOW DO YOU LOOK AFTER YOUR WELL-BEING?

It's not perfection but positive management of life.

Katrina lived a healthful life, looking after herself well with good organic food, practising yoga and meditation daily, working in a stimulating job as a university academic and generally approaching life with optimism and joy.

Just being in her company and experiencing her smiling energy made other people feel happy.

She truly approached the challenges of life with the expectation that all would eventually be well, even creating her personal mantra, 'All things turn out for the best.'

But life can throw us some curveballs at times — and Katrina had had her share of difficulties. Her husband of forty years had suffered from all manner of serious ailments through which she had nursed him over the years; her elderly parents seemed to need her support very frequently and she made herself freely available to assist her four children and five grandchildren often. She once remarked that she had spent enough time in many hospital waiting rooms and at hospital bedsides with family to know all the ins and outs of most of the city hospitals.

She continued cheerfully helping and smiling. When she herself needed two hip replacements and had a couple of falls that broke each of her ankles, she made her mind up to use the many months of immobilisation to focus on reading to satisfy her mind, daily diary writing to sustain her emotional well-being, meditation to heal her spirit, and healthy food to enrich her body. She continued to approach all her setbacks with a sense of humour and a positive healing attitude. She was amazing to all who knew her. And you would love this awesome woman for even though there were frustrating, depressing days, she just exuded a sense of well-being.

WELL-BEING QUOTIENT

The ability to nurture the whole self and live with a sense of vitality

Katrina demonstrates how well-being does not necessarily mean perfect health and peaceful living. Life can send us physical illness which debilitates us; it can lead us into stressful situations which steal our peace of mind; and it can cause us to wake up feeling like we want to slide back under the doona and make the world disappear.

None of us can be perfectly well in every aspect of our lives all the time. That is why this 'well-being' concept is almost impossible to achieve. Therefore, the best we can hope for is to manage our lives as positively as possible so that we can feel a sense of well-being to a greater or lesser degree at different stages of our lives. We can all find ways to enhance our body, mind, heart and spirit to give vitality to our energy and life force (known as *Chi* in Chinese or *Prana* in Hindu).

The ability to discover how we as individuals can nurture these aspects of ourselves, in spite of what happens to us, is the key to creating our own sense of well-being throughout our lives.

It may be that we need to cry from the deep spaces of our hearts sometimes or we feel compelled to scream from the hilltops, and on occasions, we may just curl up in bed some days. At other times, we can breathe deeply into the ocean waves or hug someone we love for as long as needed.

This is all part of self-nurturing which helps our well-being. Each of us has to discover what it is that keeps us whole — stops us from falling apart at times — and helps us to pick ourselves up, regenerate our mind, body, heart and spirit and turn our face into the storm one day and into the sunshine the next.

When our Well-being Quotient is low, there are strategies that can be helpful to switch our life force into a more positive energetic space

SWITCH STRATEGIES:
MIND. BODY. HEART. SPIRIT

MIND. What an incredible organ is the brain which controls our mind and our thinking, and what a struggle it is at times to nurture our mind so that it doesn't take over our whole being and lead us into dark territory. Our body's amazing computer allows us to view our multifaceted world and to make sense of what we see, hear, touch, smell and taste. In nurturing the well-being of our mind, one of our best strategies is *Conscious Reflection* which we can use to monitor our thoughts and subsequent actions. This involves regularly tuning in to our thoughts and asking ourselves questions, such as 'What are my deep thoughts and feelings about what I am doing at present? Am I happy/satisfied/disappointed/relieved/angry about aspects of my life? Do I feel empowered to do as I wish, or is someone else leading me into actions I do not want to take? Can I feel relaxed when I need to wind down, or does it seem impossible to get my mind into a quiet, relaxed state? Is bedtime a beautiful drifting into a refreshing deep sleep or a time of being plagued by a "monkey mind" which keeps me awake in frustration, twirling issues around in my head?' When we increase our awareness of what our mind is doing, we can understand what it is we need to do if our mind's well-being is fractured.

BODY. What a miracle the human body is and how skilled it is at communicating with us! It tells us when we feel joyful with its adrenaline surges; it heals our injuries when possible; it responds to our instant commands to spring into action as we engage with life in so many ways. It is awesome! Of course, we all know that it needs to be nurtured with good nutritional food and attention to its condition through exercise, bathing and sleeping. Unfortunately, some people do not look after its magic essence, and they constantly test its strength with harmful substances, over-indulgence in non-nutritious foods or long hours of inactive sitting and neglect. Unfortunately, many people know what they are doing and that it is possibly shortening their life, but they struggle to change the way they take care of this precious package that takes us so far.

HEART. How precious is the beating heart centre of our body! Another incredible part of us as human beings. There has been much research into the heart as a centre of feeling rather than just being labelled a life-saving pump system in the body. There is no doubt that when we feel something deeply, it often seems to emanate from the area in the body which contains the heart. It is a powerful symbol of loving feelings, heartfulness and goodness in our lives. The heart relies on the mind and body for its health and wellness, but all three work in combination to bring an overall state of well-being.

SPIRIT. If we believe that there is some greater energy within and around us (and this does not necessarily mean a concept of a religious god), we may also consider the powerful influence of what we call spirit, that seemingly invisible element that can be an inner guidance system related to our intuition. So many authors, film-makers, spiritual leaders, indigenous shamans and yogis have written of the capacity for the spirit within us to connect with universal energy and influence our health and well-being. A most fascinating book by Dr Joe Dispenza called Becoming Supernatural reveals his long research quest to scientifically record and analyse the ability of human biology to transform through self-healing techniques. Dispenza and many others, Brandon Bays among them, have shown ways to help us communicate with our own body and connect it with spiritual energy for healing. To some, it seems weird and way out, but even mainstream medical organisations are beginning to embrace 'that which cannot be explained'. Adelaide Hospital in South Australia is using aboriginal healers in its outpatient clinic and the medical staff are working together with mutual respect.

IDEAS FOR INCREASING OUR WELL-BEING

- **Relaxation techniques** such as meditation, yoga, massage, water bathing, music, playing and listening, dancing, comfortable resting, short naps, and walks in nature.

- **Distraction techniques** such as physical exercise, fun puzzles, hobbies, comedy and feel-good films, phone and skype conversations with friends, meetups with people, exercising with animals, and playing with pets.

- **Treats** such as sitting by the fire with a hot drink, eating and savouring something delicious, celebrating even small things, enjoying a sleep-in.

- **Help-Seeking** such as talking through issues with a close friend or family member, finding a professional counsellor, and consulting with doctors.

- **Internet Searching** such as googling information on a problem or anything of interest, watching helpful webinars, enjoying YouTube clips, and engaging with social media of a positive nature.

- **Life Planning** through brainstorming, mind mapping, visualization, diary writing and daydreaming.

28

X. X Factor Quotient

HOW DO YOU EXPLORE AND EXPRESS YOUR SPECIAL CHARACTERISTICS AND ABILITIES?

Mysterious qualities combine

We have all marvelled at someone we have met who just seems to have the knack for inspiring and influencing people. This kind of person seems to have it all going for them. They seem to have what we call the X Factor.

As well as their talents, actors George Clooney and Angelina Jolie have the X Factor with their conventional good looks, while singers such as Pink, Lady Gaga and Boy George have it despite deliberate unconventional looks.

Outstanding business leaders such as Steve Jobs and Elon Musk, together with politicians like Jacinda Ardern (New Zealand) and the late Bob Hawke (Australia), all reveal characteristics of the X Factor. World influential figures like Gandhi, Nelson Mandela and The Dalai Lama resonate through history for their life philosophies, while scientists and mild activists like David Attenborough and Stephen Hawking have all made a difference to our world.

In their special realms of influence, Chef Jamie Oliver and wildlife warrior Steve Irwin gained success through their enthusiasm and passion that brought their X Factor personalities forward to inspire many millions of people.

These are well-known people of influence, many of whom have changed the world for good.

X FACTOR QUOTIENT

A quality that is hard to describe that makes someone special

The X Factor is easily recognisable but fiendishly difficult to define. It may be one major factor in combination with other characteristics or a whole melting pot of personality factors that come together to create a charismatic individual who becomes influential in their particular field of endeavour.

It is fairly rare; but for those who have the X Factor, there is a world of possibilities to be explored.

While most of us do not have the X Factor, it does not mean that we cannot use what we know of this phenomenon to inform us of certain characteristics that we can improve in ourselves to give us more influence and confidence in our work and personal lives. Even if we do not acquire this factor, we can consciously develop our own 'specialness' to bring favourable outcomes into our lives.

If we reflect on the kind of qualities we may find in a person with the X Factor and develop some awareness of the extent of our own similar characteristics, we can switch up our similarities and improve our influence and popularity

SWITCH STRATEGIES: CONFIDENCE. CREATIVITY. COMPETENCE. CONNECTIONS

Confidence. People with the X Factor are naturally confident in their knowledge and able to present their ideas to a wide range of people. Confidence can be cultivated if we practise many of the strategies in this book. The keys to feeling good about ourselves lie in being less focused on worrying about what other people think and say about us and more concerned with how we feel about ourselves. If we feel our appearance, understanding of the world, ability to connect with others and capacity for receiving recognition and love are acceptable to us, in the words of Shakespeare's Hamlet, we can face 'the slings and arrows of outrageous fortune'. Any personal criticism can be used as feedback for self-improvement if we view it as having any truth; otherwise, we can dismiss it and keep our own self-belief strong. Confidence can be practiced by self-talk which affirms our worthwhileness and by facing challenging situations small steps at a time. A confident person feels valued without the arrogance of someone who knows all and refuses to listen to others. Arrogance repels people while confidence is attractive to others.

Creativity. If we meet someone who has the X Factor, he or she is often a creative thinker who can construct many ideas when needed. Whether it is a business idea or creative problem solving, these people are often the entrepreneurs who get things happening for themselves or for the organisations with which they engage. The chapter on creativity gives ideas for improving our skills here but there is no doubt some people have this attribute way beyond ordinary people, and this cannot always be acquired, for true creatives are usually born that way.

Competence in their chosen area of passionate interest and endeavour is a reason for admiration, and this is where acquiring vast knowledge and expertise is necessary for success in the work sphere of life. However, there are many who may have the elusive X Factor in their social world and career world and some who have it in only one area of their lives. Mark Zuckerberg, the Facebook creator, is such a person who carried people along with his vision but who was quite socially inept and lacking in personal connection skills. To acquire great competence is simple: study, learn, express knowledge and ideas, then keep learning for life.

Connections. The X Factor is all about connections and influence. When people realise that they can encourage and include others to embrace their vision, many use this power for achieving good outcomes in the world: changing attitudes towards less fortunate people in society; developing a voice for an important cause; articulating vital values for change in a social issue. Greta Thunberg, a young environmental activist, is an example of someone with an X Factor which is displayed in her passion and knowledge on climate change, yet she has Asperger's syndrome, limiting her social skills on a personal level. Despite this, she has inspired connections worldwide in her pleas to governments of every nation. For us, as individuals, taking the opportunity to connect personally and extensively on social media is a well-known way of becoming an 'Influencer'.

29

Y. 'Yes-ability' Quotient

HOW DO YOU EMBRACE POSSIBILITIES FOR ENRICHING YOUR LIFE?

Saying 'Yes' with a Leap of Faith.

Have we all not had times when we needed to say 'Yes!' to a huge decision, to a life-changing leap into a new experience? And has it not been such a challenge to decide on some huge issues that we have wrestled with because we understand there may be stressful, even devastating, consequences?

In my life so far, I have had to say 'Yes' to breaking an engagement in my twenties; 'Yes', to leaving a fabulous job in my thirties because it was sucking the life out of me; 'Yes' to ending a 20-year marriage in my forties; 'Yes' to starting my own business in my fifties; and 'Yes' to true love in my sixties.

All of these 'Yes' answers changed my life and each of these decisions came after much soul-searching.

I remember driving my car to work one Friday morning and, as every kilometre flipped over on my tripmeter, I felt more and more tearful as I came closer to the work environment that had once fulfilled all my dreams as the perfect job.

With a new ruthless and clueless CEO, it had become utterly unbearable. Just then, a song came on the car radio, and I wept as the singer's words pierced my heart: 'I don't want to do this anymore.' At that moment, I instinctively knew I had to get out! I resigned within half an hour of arriving that day and without a new job to go to — and with two teenage sons to support as a single mother.

This had been the second time in my life that I had left a job without a future plan, one after 7 years and another after 8 years of dedicated service. But I had to say 'Yes' to change, or I would have lost my soul.

And once decided, I never questioned my action, for then I may have been a victim — and I did not wish that to be in the story of my life's journey.

'YES-ABILITY' QUOTIENT.

The degree to which we can say 'yes' to a positive life.

'Yes-ability' is the capacity that we all have to create choices in our lives by taking a significant step away from our past and risking the future for possibilities that may or may not come to fruition. It is a brave step forward; not easy, but it is very empowering. Saying 'Yes' to something big in our lives can sometimes have huge consequences, but it has the potential to bring amazing opportunities for our future.

This is what we look for when we open ourselves to our 'Yes-ability'.

Learning to take the leap of faith required for these important life decisions is vital for personal growth, for health and well-being and for becoming the author and master of our life story.

To reflect on our 'Yes-ability', we may wish to consider some of the following questions:

Can I say YES to taking action when I feel stuck in an unsatisfactory life situation?

Can I say YES to changing my beliefs or attitudes if they are preventing me from living in joy?

Can I say YES to looking after myself? And YES to seeking help to look after others who need me?

Can I say YES to ignoring any self-sabotaging behaviours that impact my happiness?

Can I say YES to reaching out for help and support?

Can I say YES to walking away from someone in my life who is manipulative or personally destructive?

Can I say YES to showing vulnerability and accepting my feelings as part of change?

Can I say YES to love, to friendship and to working to improve my social connections if needed?

Can I say YES to confidence in my ability to make good things happen in my life?

Can I say YES to taking responsibility for my life — for my success, my achievements, my self-worth and my happiness?

Can I say YES to refusing to be a victim and blaming others for my life situation?

Can I say YES to writing and re-writing my own life story?

Can I be brave and say YES to new opportunities?

When our 'Yes-ability' is less than we would like it to be, we can improve it with helpful strategies.

SWITCH STRATEGIES: T.R.U.S.T.

T **Take time to consider the situation you need to change.** Weigh up the pros and cons of the benefits of saying YES to the action you are considering.

R **Responsibility for the decision is yours!** If someone manipulates or curbs your freedom to make a decision for your life, seek professional help to gain back your control over your life. No one owns you, even if someone behaves as if they do.

U **Understand the consequences of your 'YES' decision.** Be ready for the change that may result from your decision.

S **Speak to others and seek advice if unsure.**

T **Trust your instincts and follow your heart.**

30

Z. Zenith Quotient

HOW CONSCIOUSLY AWARE ARE YOU OF BEING YOUR BEST SELF?

At our zenith — our highest point of humanity

Anthony is a special person who has dedicated his life to self-development through education, higher study, reading, meditative practices and adventure travel.

His generosity of spirit has evolved through contributing to the betterment of individuals and organisations whenever the opportunity presents itself. He truly exudes loving, generous energy to those around him and has, as a result, become one of the best, most evolved human beings I know.

He may be considered to be truly close to his Zenith or best self, but by the very application he directs towards being his best, he continues to believe that he can still be more and better than he is at present. Paradoxically, by enriching himself through deeper understanding of and generosity to others, he spreads loving energy in the world and in return, receives it back in gratitude for a life well-lived. But he does so with humility, for he views himself as an ordinary person. Even though he may give money to needy people, as many of us do, it is his interest in talking to them, asking them about their story and caring for strangers that inspires me.

He is not afraid to get involved in helping others, especially the powerless. An unwell tourist who became stranded in India was assisted financially by Anthony to return home for medical care. A distressed elderly lady with dementia, standing dazed on the street was calmed by him taking time to make phone calls for help and waiting till the situation was resolved. A man who collapsed in a restaurant, having fits, was reassured by Anthony sitting on the ground and speaking gently while waiting for the ambulance. This is a caring human being who is there for friends and strangers alike — a person who sees himself as imperfect but who emanates loving energy.

When people are in the presence of the Dalai Lama, they usually 'feel' his calm, gentle wisdom, and when Gandhi transformed India, he did so by encouraging only peaceful protests and remaining in a state of loving energy, even up to the tragic moment of his assassination. There are other world figures who could be named here, and many of us know of someone who has this presence of deep humanity within their being.

How enriching is it to be in the company of a person who emanates an energy of warm, positive love and generosity as a way of daily living. It is rare to find such people, as it is understandable for us all to be weighed down by worries at times or to become disheartened with troubles that rest heavily upon us. If we think about people we have known or simply met in our lives, we may have been impressed by the particular qualities of some of these human beings.

ZENITH QUOTIENT

The quality of raising our awareness and actions to their highest level so that we can live our best life. More than this, though, i s the capacity for the generosity of spirit and love to be a guidance system for life

It is a challenge to wake up and 'shine' on many of our 'life days' and although as human beings we cannot expect to feel happy and confident every day, by increasing our conscious awareness of the state of our body, mind, heart and spirit, we can accept and re-create our life journey each day along the way. By taking responsibility for how we approach life, we also gain control over our individual life stories. When we become aware that we are blaming others or waiting for someone to rescue us from our misery, we can decide to Switch our perspective and change our story.

To become an evolved human being and reach our Zenith state requires an attitude of loving generosity to others, a commitment to personal growth, a highly developed capacity for self-reflection and the insight to understand personal responsibility for our lives.

I vividly remember at a workshop given by Kevin Billet on his book *Light in the Heart of Darkness*, a participant complained agonisingly about how the destructive power of her mother's manipulation had 'ruined' her life. After she declared that she would never be happy, Kevin asked her why she didn't cut off contact with her mother if her emotional life was in peril. Her reply that she couldn't walk away from her mother because she was connected by family ties, drew the direct observation from Kevin that this choice to do nothing was a choice that would keep her in misery.

By implication, although he did not say this, he seemed to be suggesting that she didn't want to rescue herself from this situation because she would have to write a different story which did not include being a victim'. While this seems harsh, it gave the woman a different response from the usual sympathy she sought but which had so far not resulted in change or resolution of the problem. Consciously reflecting on the themes and dramas of our own life story can help us to choose a different road on our journey and to learn how, as the saying goes, when life gives us 'lemons', we can make 'lemonade'.

How can we Switch our actions to live our best life in a Zenith state even if, at times, life challenges?

SWITCH STRATEGIES TO REACH OUR ZENITH EXISTENCE

We are happier as human beings...

- If we love ourselves and others for all the amazing talents and quotients with which we are blessed.

- If we celebrate the small successes as well as the grand achievements of ourselves and others.

- If we give our best effort to all the small and large things we do.

- If we hold ourselves back from complaining about what is wrong and search for what is right in the world.

- If we feel acceptance of who we are and of other human beings we meet who, like us, are trying to live their best lives.

- If we rise above the criticisms of others who have a less generous spirit than us and, by valuing ourselves, refrain from the habit of criticising.

- If we approach living with the desire to understand rather than to condemn.

- If we praise and recognise effort and enthusiasm both in ourselves and others.

- If we receive help with great gratitude and, in return, reach out to support others with a generous heart.

- If we wake up and, even when we feel low or sad, we can release these feelings and let them float into forgetfulness with time, enough to find something positive in each day.

- If we remember how fortunate we are to be reading this when people in so many places in the world live in poverty and hunger, unable to read, yet they can often smile more readily than many of us.
- If we find love and joy with other humans or with warm, huggy pets.
- If we sit at times in peacefulness and prayer, especially in nature, and allow our spirit to be refreshed.
- If we raise our energy, our essential life force, by doing helpful, generous things for others so they feel good, and we also feel the pleasure of giving.
- If we turn on our joyful music and remember to do our happy dance or open a paint box and fill our world with colour.
- If we remind ourselves to live our best lives in loving energy by whispering to our hearts that we have much to be grateful for and life is worth living for every magical sunrise.

31

Blessings

With great hopefulness, my wish is that there may be a message or two within this book for all who read it in part or as a whole. May we always remember that the future begins now, in this moment, and it is always open for any possibilities — for anything wonderful to come and change our life's journey into great goodness.

SWITCH IT

Switch on our ATTITUDE to live our life's best

Switch up our BRAVERY when anxious and stressed

Switch on CREATIVITY to find what we need

Switch DETERMINATION from 'can't' to 'succeed'

Switch up EMPATHY to know others' feelings

Switch on FORGIVENESS to allow for our healing

Switch into GROWTH mode so sorrow brings knowing

Switch up HEARTFULNESS when love needs growing

Switch to INTUITION if uncertainty arises

Switch to JOY when life surprises

Switch on KNOWLEDGE to show people how

Switch up LAUGHTER instead of a growl

Switch into MINDFULNESS when so much needs doing

Switch to NEUTRALITY when anger is brewing

Switch up OPTIMISM if hope is fading

Switch on PASSION for energy upgrading

Switch on QUESTIONABILITY to know people's thinking

Switch up RESILIENCY when you feel your heart sinking

Switch up SOCIABILITY for friendships to flow

Switch on THANKFULNESS for happiness to grow

Switch on UNDERSTANDING to know how you're feeling

Switch on VISUALIZATION for future revealing

Switch up WELL-BEING for feeling the zest

Switch on X FACTORS to rise with the best

Switch YES-ABILITY from no to go

Switch life to ZENITH for life to flow.

BLESSINGS TO YOU FOR LIVING JOYFULLY AND SEEKING YOUR OWN WAY...

Contact Rhonda at
youswitchit@gmail.com

www.ingramcontent.com/pod-product-compliance
Lightning Source LLC
Chambersburg PA
CBHW050311010526
44107CB00055B/2198